Praise for
Transforming The Living Legacy of Trauma

"Reading Janina Fisher's wonderful, generous, and beautifully written *Transforming The Living Legacy of Trauma* reminds me of how much we, as a profession, have learned in only three short decades. This book beautifully articulates how mind and body adapt to intolerable feelings of terror, self-loathing, and fear of abandonment with a range of ingenious solutions to create some semblance of safety and control. These adaptations endure over time, and eventually tend to interfere with having satisfying relationships with one's self and others. Janina shows us that healing traumatic wounds consists of learning new habits of observation and self-discovery. The goal of treatment is not so much digging up the past but the repair of the injuries suffered as a result of traumatizing experiences. It's a marvelous and easily accessible work that should be part of every therapist's skill set."

— **Bessel van der Kolk, MD,** President, Trauma Research Foundation
Professor of psychiatry, Boston University School of Medicine
author of *New York Times* bestseller *The Body Keeps the Score*

"Written with her characteristic hopefulness and clarity, this outstanding workbook showcases Janina Fisher's unique gift of getting to the essence of things. Complex theories are transformed into simple, easily understood, useful concepts that teach clients to make sense of their symptoms, to befriend their coping strategies, and to practice effective skills to relieve their suffering. Perhaps even more noteworthy, this remarkable book will inspire the confidence that healing is possible for even the most traumatized survivor."

— **Pat Ogden, PhD,** author of *Sensorimotor Psychotherapy: Interventions for Trauma and Attachment* and *The Pocket Guide to Sensorimotor Psychotherapy*

"Fisher brings the most important concepts of trauma recovery to life—in both words and diagrams—with simultaneous simplicity and sophistication. She has a knack for communicating complex trauma-related ideas and information in an economical and easy-to-understand way. And, as always, she offers her readers hope and invaluable practical guidance.

With its easy-to-understand diagrams, powerful case examples, and crystal-clear explanations of complex concepts, this book belongs on every therapist's (and not just trauma therapists) and survivor's bookshelf. Fisher reaches out to her readers with compassion and encouragement, offering a unique guide to comprehensive healing.

Fisher's diagrams and worksheets are being used all over the world by therapists and survivors. They are a valued part of my personal trauma treatment toolbox. In this book, she effectively couples these materials with user-friendly explanations and case examples, bringing them fully to life for the reader. All I can say is wow!"

— **Deborah Korn, PsyD,** The EMDR Institute, author of
Every Memory Deserves Respect: EMDR, the Proven Trauma Therapy with the Power to Heal

"In this succinct and well-organized volume, Janina Fisher distills the essence of modern trauma theory and the deep wisdom of her decades of clinical experience. The result is a welcome, reader-friendly primer for personal use or to support professional work with trauma survivors."

— **Gabor Maté, MD,** author of
In The Realm of Hungry Ghosts: Close Encounters With Addiction

"Renowned trauma recovery pioneer, Janina Fisher offers a superb, user friendly, and comprehensive guide to healing for all trauma survivors and for therapists as well. Grounded in expert knowledge of neurobiological, *Transforming the Legacy of Trauma* walks readers step-by-step through an effective process of deep, lasting change, looking both at childhood injuries and at lifelong adaptations to them. Practical, smart, and wise, this book has the power to change your life."

— **Terry Real**, author of
The New Rules of Marriage and founder of the Relational Life Institute

"This workbook is an extraordinary gift for therapists and clients alike. With her trademark compassion, Dr. Fisher succeeds in de-pathologizing and simplifying the complexities of the cognitive, somatic, emotional, and behavioral residue of trauma. Clients will be tremendously enlightened as they learn about the brain's ability to process, store, and remember trauma, how to identify and navigate triggers and destructive coping strategies, the impact of disorganized attachment and dissociation, and how to distinguish an unsafe past from an empowered present. The visual aids make essential information readily accessible while the worksheets and "parts" perspective replace self-blame and shame with newfound insight, curiosity, self-compassion, and genuine healing. An absolute must-read for every therapist who wants to be trauma informed, and a life-changing workbook for trauma survivors!"

— **Lisa Ferentz**, author of
Letting Go of Self-Destructive Behaviors: A Workbook of Hope and Healing

"Janina Fisher has contributed meaningfully to trauma recovery in this wonderful workbook. With her up-to-date approaches, practical techniques and worksheets to help guide healing, this book is a must have for resolving deeply-held trauma responses. I highly recommend it."

— **Nancy J. Napier, LMFT**, author of
Getting Through the Day, Recreating Your Self, and *Sacred Practices for Conscious Living*

"Janina Fisher and I have long followed parallel paths promoting greater attention to stabilization in trauma therapy. Here she furthers her careful, educational, common sense, and resource-rich approach, filling a much-neglected niche in the trauma self-help literature. Fisher successfully balances illuminating commonalities of post traumatic conditions while encouraging readers to select, portion, and pace individualized healing paths. This book provides an excellent adjunct to any course of trauma therapy or personal self-help."

— **Babette Rothschild**, author of
The Body Remembers, Vols. 1 & 2 (2000 & 2017) & *8 Keys to Safe Trauma Recovery* (2010)

Transforming the
Living Legacy of Trauma

A Workbook For
Survivors and Therapists

Janina Fisher, PhD

Published by
PESI Publishing & Media
PESI, Inc.
3839 White Ave
Eau Claire, WI 54703

Cover: Amy Rubenzer
Editing: Miriam Ramos
Layout: Amy Rubenzer & Bookmasters

ISBN: 9781683733485
Printed in the United States of America

PESI
Publishing
& Media
pesipublishing.com

ABOUT THE AUTHOR

Janina Fisher, PhD, is the assistant educational director of the Sensorimotor Psychotherapy Institute and a former instructor at Harvard Medical School. An international expert on the treatment of trauma, she is the author of *Healing the Fragmented Selves of Trauma Survivors: Overcoming Self-Alienation* and is co-author with Pat Ogden of *Sensorimotor Psychotherapy: Interventions for Attachment and Trauma*. She is known for her work on integrating neuroscience research and newer body-centered interventions into traditional psychotherapy approaches. More information can be found on her website: www.janinafisher.com.

TABLE OF CONTENTS

Chapter

WORKSHEETS

ACKNOWLEDGMENTS

It takes a village to write a book, and I am grateful to all the villagers whose work has made mine possible. First, I want to thank the leaders of the trauma treatment village, Bessel van der Kolk and Judith Herman. Without their inspiration, determination, and unrelenting commitment, we would not have a trauma treatment field or a worldwide community of trauma specialists today. I first was inspired to devote my professional life to trauma when I heard Judith Herman speak in 1989, and I still remember the words that changed the course of my career aspirations. She said, "Doesn't it make more sense that people suffer because of real things that have happened to them than that they suffer because of their infantile fantasies or their mental 'illness?'" It did make sense that real things had happened to my clients—real and terrible things.

The other words that changed the course of my life and work came from Bessel van der Kolk: "The body keeps the score," he asserted in 1994. Had he not had the courage to say something that, at the time, was considered crazy, the field would never have discovered the neurobiological source of what I call "the living legacy of trauma." Without his encouragement and mentorship, I would never have become a voice for integrating these new ideas into trauma treatment. Bessel, thank you from the bottom of my heart for making possible the privilege of doing what I do.

Had it not been for Pat Ogden and Sensorimotor Psychotherapy, I would not have known how to work with the body as well as the mind; would not have had the opportunity to learn such a gentle, nonviolent treatment for trauma; and I would not have had the incredible opportunities that Pat has generously made possible.

But, most of all, if it had not been for the clients who have been my teachers since the 1990s, I would never have come to understand trauma as I do. I would not be able to speak for trauma survivors without having had such gifted and generous teachers. I wish I could name you all by name, but I hope you know who you are. Each one of you has taught me something reflected in this book.

I want to acknowledge my fellow "villagers" scattered all over the world. Their support for me personally and for the mission we share has been invaluable. In Italy, Giovanni Tagliavini and Paola Boldrini, beloved friends and fellow travelers in this field, have worked tirelessly to improve the understanding of trauma and dissociation and to create a community for Italian trauma therapists. Trine Anstorp and Kirsten Benum, my wonderful Norwegian family of friends, have devoted their entire professional lives to improving the understanding of trauma in Norway. In Australia, my good friend Naomi Halpern has worked tirelessly for over 20 years to bring cutting edge trauma training to Australian therapists.

Writers also need friends and colleagues who are willing to nag, coax, encourage, and then nag us some more until we finally get the book done. Dear friends Stephanie Ross and Deborah Spragg are always my best naggers, reminding me frequently that I have something to say and that it is about time I said it. Deirdre Fay always had the vision for what I could do long before I could see it, and I am deeply grateful that she finally convinced me to believe her! Lisa Ferentz has always been my book-writing maven and role model. My thanks to her and to our power women, Denise Tordella and Robyn Brickel. Thank you to Terry Trotter, Sally LoGrasso, Phyllis Lorenz, Ellen Odza, Marilynne Chophel, and the rest of my Bay Area Sensorimotor Psychotherapy community for being such very vocal encouragers. And then there is the younger generation: My thanks to Maren Masino for making my work better and always reminding me that I have something to say that needs saying.

An author invariably needs other eyes and ears to help communicate on paper what is so clear in her mind. My thanks to Audrey Fortin for reading portions of this manuscript and giving me such very helpful feedback and to Linda Jackson, my publisher, for her unwavering support over many years. I am also deeply grateful to John Braman for his wise, mindfully-informed guidance in all things.

A very, very special note of gratitude to my amazing and gifted editor, Miriam Ramos, whose attention to detail helped to make this book far better than the one I first wrote. Her therapist mind always saw what needed to be said more clearly, while her editorial eye caught every error and repetition.

And then, last but hardly least, I want to thank my family: Jadu and Wendy, Jason and Kelli, and my amazing granddaughters Ruby and Nika. Thank you for always being there, for taking such good care of your aging mama and grandmother, and for putting up with this book! Writing a book is always a family sacrifice. My love and my heartfelt thanks to all of you.

TRAUMA SURVIVORS

HOW TO USE THIS BOOK

This book was written for you.

Even though you are not responsible for the traumatic events you endured, you have been left to manage all the challenges of recovering from those experiences. Worse yet, there is no road map for understanding how you are affected by what happened or to guide you in recovering. That is the purpose of this book—to provide you with a map and detailed directions for the journey ahead based on the latest understanding of trauma and its effects.

Thirty years ago, it was thought that traumatic experiences could be healed when the secrets were finally revealed and the story of what happened was told to a safe, validating witness. However, contrary to what we believed then, that process often made the traumatic effects worse instead of better. I remember thinking at the time how unfair that was. Why should it take more suffering to heal from what someone had already suffered? No one else seemed to question it because it was the only map we possessed in the 1990s, even if it was not getting survivors any closer to the destination they wished to reach.

My first teacher in the field of trauma, Judith Herman, believed something different: She was adamant that what survivors needed was information. They needed to be educated about trauma and all its ramifications and manifestations. They needed to know enough to make intelligent choices about their lives and treatment. It was important, she said, for survivors to be full collaborators with the therapist rather than passive recipients of therapy. As victims of trauma, they had been disempowered and deprived of choice. The antidote, said Judith Herman, was the power of knowledge, some way to understand the baffling and intense reactions that had plagued them, often for years, so they did not feel so crazy and abnormal. However, there was one problem. As you will read in Chapter One, threat and danger automatically shut down the part of the brain that has the ability to think, plan, and remember. Thinking takes too long; instinctive survival responses are quicker. The body operates on the principle that it is better to start running now than to stand around wondering how to get out of danger.

You might have noticed that new information, even if reassuring, is difficult for you to process. That is because a traumatized brain, conditioned by years of abuse, shuts down each time you are triggered, every time you feel vulnerable, threatened, or even hear someone say the word *trauma*. In trying to find ways to get around this problem, I discovered that it helped to draw pictures of what I was trying to explain. These simple images seemed to wake up the thinking brain and, suddenly, it would become possible to focus more easily. Even adolescents found it easy to understand information about the brain and nervous system when it was communicated by way of these simple diagrams.

This workbook was written to support you, with or without the help of a therapist, and to educate therapists and survivors together about the latest understanding of trauma and its effects on the body and brain. Although I would recommend using this book with a trauma-informed therapist, it can also be used entirely on your own. Not all survivors have access to specialized trauma treatment or sometimes to any treatment at all. Either way, having a guidebook that you can use on your own has many benefits, too, even when you have the availability of a skilled therapist.

One of the many consequences of trauma is a loss of trust in human beings. Fear of vulnerability, a phobia of dependence, fear of self-disclosure, and careful avoidance of sadness and anger are also common symptoms. Each of these fears is adaptive in a world in which even a child's caretakers are not to be trusted, where tears or anger are punished, emotional needs are exploited, and dependence is dangerous. But having had these experiences makes trauma therapy very challenging. We cannot avoid all vulnerability in therapy; we cannot prevent perfectly normal feelings of dependency or the wish to depend from spontaneously coming up; we cannot outlaw tears or anger.

Therapists understandably want their clients to trust without always realizing how difficult it is to trust anyone when every instinct in your body is saying, "Danger, danger—do not believe this person—do not trust." I found that education about trauma helped my clients because it gave them factual information coming from research and writing. I was not asking them to trust me or my opinions. I was asking them to trust facts. Trusting information was much easier for most of them than trusting me as a person. They felt validated by the diagrams and relieved to learn that their actions and reactions were normal ones. And the more often I gave my clients copies of these diagrams as homework, the more it seemed to help them stay centered and stable between weekly therapy sessions.

This is the threefold intention of the workbook: to help you make sense of your most confusing, puzzling, and even shameful symptoms; to support your recovery by providing you with ways to recognize the living legacy of traumatic experience as it affects your day-to-day life; and to practice new habits of response.

SOME SUGGESTIONS FOR HOW TO USE THIS BOOK

This book is not a book about dealing with traumatic memories. It is intended to help you recover from the *effects* of trauma: the physical effects, the emotional effects, and the changes in belief it creates. You may not yet know all the ways in which you have been affected by your trauma, but I encourage you to assume that any highly distressing or overwhelming emotion that you do not understand might be a trauma symptom. Consider the possibility that self-destructive impulses, critical or fearful thoughts, or feelings of numbness or disconnection might also be the effects of trauma. I have found that trauma survivors suffer from too much emotion, even if they cannot feel it. Having no emotion at all is the reaction of the body to feelings that exceed our ability to tolerate. If you are alive, then you are feeling—even if you are numb and cut off from your emotions or your body.

Take your time with this book. It will not be helpful if it overwhelms you or shuts you down. Do not feel that you have to read the whole thing, and do assume that feeling pressure to rush through it is probably trauma-related. I would advise reading a chapter at a time, taking some days or weeks to make sense of that section, doing one worksheet, seeing how that feels, then trying another one. If a worksheet is helpful, make several copies and keep filling them out, especially when times are challenging for you. The right ones can be a way to keep your head on straight, to help you stay centered and know where you are. If a worksheet is too triggering or makes it hard to think, just put it aside and leave it for another time, or skip it completely.

You do not have to get an A in this course! This book was designed to be your ally in healing—not another pressure or burden or goal.

Do more of what speaks to you, and give yourself permission to do less with sections that are more difficult or less relevant. A workbook inevitably includes information that is very timely and relevant to you, as well as information that seems too obvious or simply unrelated to what you are experiencing. Instead of trying to go through the book section by section, in the order in which it is written, give yourself permission to pick and choose. Learning to pay attention to what you need in the moment is an important skill in recovery.

But also, be curious if you have strong negative reactions to certain sections in this book. Without putting yourself under pressure to figure out why, assume that a strong negative reaction means that some fear or trauma-related resistance has been triggered. Resistance should never be considered a negative reaction—it simply means that we feel threatened, and being curious about any feelings of threat or danger is always illuminating. It does not mean that you have to address those sections—just be curious about your mistrust or aversion. If you can, try out worksheets even if you do not like them. Give them a "test drive" to see if they are as bad as you think. Try out things you do not like and see if they help. If they do not, or if they are overwhelming, give yourself permission to go on to something else. You can always return to skipped sections or worksheets later and see if they have gotten any more relevant or less difficult.

Remember that traumatic effects and symptoms are not something you asked for or something you can control. However, understanding them will help you live more comfortably in your own skin.

Trauma impacts human beings in very specific ways because we have a brain and body designed to prioritize survival. Our bodies and brains adapt to trauma by instinctively developing anticipatory patterns meant to protect us against the same dangers repeating themselves again. If you are feeling overwhelmed or tortured by the symptoms (depression, hopelessness, flashbacks, fears and phobias, fears of abandonment and/or closeness), remind yourself that each of these reactions represents a survival strategy. Flashbacks keep us on guard; depression and hopelessness shut us down so we are better at being seen but not heard; fear restricts our relationships and our freedom to act; shame makes us retreat into invisibility. Each symptom represents a way your brain and body adapted to a chronic condition of threat. When you are frustrated by the living legacy of trauma, blame your brain and your nervous system, not yourself!

Never push yourself or try too hard—but do not give up either. Because survival is an effort, because it includes being pushed to the limits and having to "keep on keeping on," healing should be as easy as possible. Giving up is not healing. Neither is self-judgment. But making a choice to go slowly and easily, to never force anything, to challenge yourself without pressure or judgment, are important principles in healing work. There is no right or wrong way to use this workbook. Faced with something you long to avoid, take your time to be curious about the impulse to avoid, wonder about it, and then make a thoughtful choice about tackling it versus following your impulse to ignore it. You might decide to ignore it for now, tackle it to see what is so threatening, or just pass over that section.

Last but not least, I wish you well on your journey toward healing and recovery. My professional mission for almost 40 years has been to increase international awareness and understanding of trauma and to support treatments that resolve the post-traumatic living legacy with which trauma survivors are burdened long after they have survived.

I am glad you survived, and now it is time to heal. I hope this workbook will help you on the way.

THERAPISTS

HOW YOU AND YOUR CLIENTS CAN USE THIS BOOK

Transforming the Living Legacy of Trauma was inspired by the ideas of the two most influential pioneers in the trauma field: Judith Herman and Bessel van der Kolk. I was fortunate enough to have Judy Herman as a teacher in the early 1990s and even more fortunate to have Bessel as a long-time colleague/mentor beginning in 1995, just at the start of the neurobiological revolution that transformed our ideas about what it means to treat a trauma. Research on traumatic memory, inspired by Bessel van der Kolk's theory that "the body keeps the score," helped to change the direction of the field from event-centered to experience-centered, from emotion-centered to brain-centered. As the goals of trauma therapy transformed and as we better understood the long-term impact of traumatic experiences, it became increasingly clear that new approaches were needed—approaches that felt less overwhelming and more empowering for those we were trying to help.

But it was not just the leaders and pioneers who changed the direction of the trauma treatment field—it was also the survivors.

Focused on retrieving memories of events and sharing these stories with a non-judgmental witness, the early treatments for trauma never had the effect therapists and clients initially hoped. Traumatized clients taught us that telling their stories was not the relief they were led to expect. The overwhelming emotions evoked were not consistently of therapeutic value because they exceeded most individuals' capacity to feel. Telling the story and feeling their emotional responses was often experienced as re-traumatizing and disturbing rather than healing. Many individuals did not recall the stories they told because they could not speak of the events and stay present at the same time. Many more could not feel or remember being witnessed. Judith Herman was very alarmed by what she observed in her clients as they told their stories. Some became more self-destructive and suicidal, began using drugs and alcohol to manage their overwhelming feelings, or could no longer function. She was adamant that treatment for trauma should not cause more suffering or further disrupt the lives of those who had suffered so much.

So, like many of the early leaders in the field, she turned to an idea first proposed by Dr. Pierre Janet in the late 1800s: a phase-oriented treatment model in which client and therapist concentrated first on stabilizing the symptoms and emotions, developing a foundation for clients that would allow them to address the traumatic past from a position of strength (Herman, 1992). As a feminist, she was particularly attentive to issues of power and privilege, and, concerned about the inherent inequality of the therapeutic relationship, she developed an approach that began with educating the survivor to become an expert on trauma. The goal was to equalize the balance of power by equalizing knowledge: If the survivors knew what the therapist knew, then they could be more like equals in trauma work. In 1990, this was a radical idea. In that era, psychoeducation had no place in the psychotherapy world. It was considered too intellectual—it was not therapy.

Nonetheless, as a postdoctoral fellow in Judith Herman's clinic, I was expected to learn how to provide psychoeducation that would normalize the feelings and symptoms that tormented my clients. Normalizing their suicidality, their self-harm, their hopelessness, their tendency to isolate, their mistrust, and their fear of abandonment would lessen the shame, she believed, and help them to experience themselves as ingenious survivors instead of humiliated victims. It was not always easy, but I rarely encountered clients who objected to this education as long as it was embedded in empathy—not so much empathy for their vulnerability but empathy for how they had survived. Psychoeducation made it easier to tolerate acknowledging what they had been through without having to explore all the details and reexperience the overwhelming emotions. It made it easier to hope, made it easier to believe they could recover. After all, they *had* survived!

The next important lesson I learned was in Bessel van der Kolk's clinic. The focus at his clinic was not so much on specific events but on the cumulative impact on young children of separation and attachment failure, neglect, abuse, and domestic violence. It was rare for our clients to have had one single traumatic event. Most had endured multiple events at the hands of several different perpetrators in a context of neglect and attachment failure. As a supervisor sitting in on Bessel's clinical team meetings, I was privy each week to the new information about the nature of trauma that emerged as a result of the first brain scan research studies. His first study on the nature of traumatic memory demonstrated that, when subjects recalled a traumatic event, the prefrontal cortex (especially the areas in the left hemisphere responsible for verbal memory and expression) became inactive, while nonverbal areas of the brain (the limbic system, specifically the amygdala) become highly active. In other words, these individuals lost their ability to remember in words and began remembering physically and emotionally. The research finally made sense as to why so many of our clients had traumatic amnesia for the events they had experienced and why, at the same time, they were so symptomatic. They were experiencing their trauma as sensory fragments without words (van der Kolk & Fisler, 1995, p. 516), divorced from any chronological memory of the event.

These nonverbal, sensory elements of the traumatic experiences were sometimes the only record left of what had happened, constituting a living legacy that could not be resolved because the feelings and physical reactions did not feel past—they felt very present, here and now. Even the client's symptoms, the very reasons for seeking treatment, were usually evidence of traumatic memory at work. Mary Harvey, Judith Herman's colleague, used to say, "Trauma survivors have symptoms instead of memories" (personal communication, September 23, 1990). Bessel van der Kolk's research was proving her correct, but most clients did not know they were remembering when they felt afraid, ashamed, enraged, or frightened. And most therapists did not know either.

In this context, it became even more important to educate my clients about their symptoms and reactions. But now psychoeducation meant trying to explain how their brains worked. And we would have to try to explain these complex concepts even though the research showed that working memory and capacity for verbal expression were impaired by the trauma responses. In order to simplify this complicated information and make it accessible to my clients, I discovered through trial and error that it helped to draw simple diagrams so that there were fewer words to process.

To my surprise, most clients could understand my "Brain Science for Dummies" approach, and they were also able to focus more easily when I depicted the concepts through the drawings than when I put them into words. In fact, the fewer words I used, the better it was for them! And then, thanks to a colleague who asked me to publish the diagrams so that she and others could use them, I created the first flip chart and named it "Psychoeducational Aids for Treating Psychological Trauma." It had to be a flip chart because psychoeducation is a collaborative task. It requires that both client and therapist be able to see the diagrams together. It had to stand up on an easel or stand so that it did not require physical closeness to see the same page, and it had to be big enough to be visible to both parties.

Ten years later, this workbook is being written to accompany the flip chart, explain the diagrams more fully, and provide some strategies for addressing trauma responses that can be used in therapy sessions or at home.

USING THE WORKBOOK WITH YOUR CLIENTS

My first and most important recommendation to the therapist is: **Slower is faster.**

Evoke the client's interest in these ideas before recommending or assigning the workbook. Psychoeducation does not have to be academic—it can be very relational. And that includes attunement to the client's state and interests. If I recommend the workbook before creating a rationale for its use, the client is less likely to actually use it. If I ignite clients' curiosity or interest, they will be motivated to explore its contents. And the easiest way to evoke curiosity is by showing the client the first flip chart diagram: "The Living Legacy of Trauma."

When I introduce the flip chart, I usually start by saying, "Can I show you something that might help you understand why things have been so difficult for you? Why you have been feeling crazy? Why it has been so overwhelming?" Then I show them the first diagram, Figure 1.1 on page 14, because it tends to be relevant to most clients' troubling issues and symptoms. Neither the flip chart nor the workbook, however, have to be used sequentially. In fact, this work has much greater therapeutic impact if it is employed as an empathic response in the moment to something troubling or baffling to the client. Luckily, the first diagram is easy to use in that way.

Because it is important that the flip chart and workbook feel relevant and relational, I suggest that therapists read the workbook first (or at least the first few chapters) so that they are familiar with the topics it addresses. That makes it easier to react spontaneously to clients' needs in the moment and to convey genuine interest or excitement about how a concept or chapter might speak to them.

The relational value of the therapist's being able to connect the client's immediate need to some relevant information in the flip chart or workbook is very powerful. Traumatized individuals have generally not had the experience of a spontaneous, attuned reaction to their feelings and needs. When we are able to make a connection between the distress clients are experiencing now and a larger context that validates or normalizes what they feel, it is very reassuring.

Carla came to her first appointment in a highly dysregulated state. She sat on the edge of her chair, agitated, trembling, speaking so fast she could barely get the words out. Confused and overwhelmed by the trauma-related responses that had suddenly begun flooding her mind and body, this high-functioning professional sought help from several different therapists, but talking about her traumatic childhood had only increased the intensity of her symptoms and emotions.

First, I had to validate and normalize her experience. I had to meet Carla where she was and educate her about what was going on. "You are flooded—that's what's wrong," I told her. "Your body and nervous system are so highly activated you cannot think straight." She agreed, "The only time I feel any relief is at work—for a few hours at least."

"Yes, that makes perfect sense," I said, validating her again. "The traumatic activation is shutting down your prefrontal cortex. You get relief at work because your job stimulates your prefrontal cortex. Can I show you?" She nodded, and I opened the flip chart to the corresponding figure and turned it to face her. Immediately, I could see her begin to focus and her body calm a bit as she did so. "The brain remembers overwhelming experiences primarily as feeling and body memories, not so much as events—that is what has been overwhelming you. You must have thought you were going crazy!" I spoke the deepest fear most trauma survivors have and then used the flip chart to reassure her. "But this is normal—because as you see here, traumatic experiences are recorded in this little area called the 'amygdala,' and that is why the symptoms are so intense. You are not getting pictures or flashbacks—you are getting these emotional and physical reactions that overwhelm you because they are traumatic memories. And then your frontal lobes shut down! So, you have all this anxiety in your body and no way to make sense of it." I could see Carla's agitation decreasing bit by bit as she listened and looked at the diagram. "You will feel better if we can keep your frontal lobes online—like they are at your job." Carla answered, "I am interested in anything that will help me stop feeling this way!"

Always wait for the client to show interest before suggesting any intervention. Traumatized individuals like Carla are very sensitive to how they are met by others, and prematurely recommending this workbook or any other intervention may actually discourage their interest. Try to find a reason coming from the client's expressed concerns that necessitates its use: "If this way of understanding trauma makes sense to you, you might be interested in the workbook that goes with this diagram..." or "If this feels validating, you might also like the workbook..." Notice that I do not directly recommend the workbook. Instead, I mention that it is a resource and leave it to the client to express some curiosity about it. Or I could just have it sitting on my coffee table so the client sees it each week and becomes curious about it. I could also refer to it as we go along: "This reminds me of something in this workbook... Can I show you?" Or I share with the client, "I have been reading this workbook and thinking that you might find it helpful—could I show you something from it?"

Remember that trauma is the experience of being forced to do what others want. It is therefore very important in trauma treatment for the therapist to offer choices, even when we feel certain in our own minds about what would help the client. Some clients will only want to read the text, whereas others will love the worksheets and be eager to use them. Some will have a negative reaction to the word *homework*, especially if they have had learning disabilities or painful educational experiences. If they fear failure or shame, you might suggest that the two of you experiment to see if a worksheet is useful. You might read a paragraph that speaks to what the client is experiencing, and then you and your client could fill out a worksheet collaboratively and see if the client finds either of any value. The less pressure we put on the client, the more collaborative the treatment will feel. The more easily we can laugh at ourselves if a diagram or worksheet is not useful and blame ourselves for guessing wrongly, the more willing most clients will be to try the material another time. And if they feel validated by the flip chart, the more willing they will be to see if the workbook is also validating.

"Bite-sizing" information is crucial. Remember the effects of traumatic activation on the thinking brain, as Carla attests. Our clients cannot process too much information at a time, so we have to give them small pieces to absorb before introducing the next piece. Each diagram presents a different concept and, in most cases, it is better to introduce only one concept per session or, at most, two related flip chart pages. "Slower is faster" is the expression I learned about trauma work early in my career, and it is a reassuring expression even for clients who are in a hurry. If I bite-size new material, the client can really take it in or get interested in it, and we will progress more quickly in the end. If I present too much information and it overwhelms the client, it will slow us down. The client may become averse to more new information or have a harder time trusting me when I want to present even more psychoeducation.

Do not be task-oriented in the use of this book. It will be of more value to the client if it is used as a resource rather than an end in itself. It is meant to support the effectiveness of any trauma treatment using any method, so it is crucial that the client experience it as a resource and an ally. The workbook can be used in the preparation phase for Eye Movement Desensitization and Reprocessing (EMDR; Shapiro, 2001) or for body-centered methods, such as Sensorimotor Psychotherapy (Ogden & Fisher, 2015) and Somatic Experiencing (Levine, 2015). It can be helpful in stabilizing clients prior to any type of trauma processing or simply in helping them regain their ability to function. If you are a therapist working with a limited number of sessions and feeling the pressure to get a lot of work done in a short time, you might introduce the book as a way of maximizing the time you have or carrying on what you and the client have started even after the ending of this phase of treatment. Stabilization and education are of even greater importance when therapists are working under short-term therapy constraints. But just keep in mind that too much information at one time will discourage, rather than inspire, the client. The goal is to equip survivors with psychoeducation that helps them manage their symptoms and triggered responses, supports their emerging life after trauma, and validates their experience without requiring that they remember all of its horrifying details.

ENGAGE THE CLIENT IN MUTUAL EXPLORATION

The workbook will have greater impact if it is connected to the therapeutic relationship. Rather than assigning the book as reading material for therapy, which can feel distancing, use it together as a shared resource or guidebook for therapy.

Remember that, as the therapist, you are more likely to have a prefrontal cortex that is not inhibited by traumatic activation. Your ability to absorb new information and generalize or apply it will be greater than the client's. Do not be afraid to help clients think about these ideas. You will not be doing the thinking for them. You will be stimulating their own brain activity. Make use of the flip chart and workbook as a shared experience. Do not hesitate to offer your personal perspective: "This is what I get from this page. You actually do not have poor judgment. Triggers shut your thinking brain down, and the feelings and impulses just take over. Does that make sense?" Or ask clients about their perspective: "Can you relate to this page? Do you notice this in your own life? How does this apply to you?" Or even: "I was thinking about how much this applies to your experience. Do you get that same feeling?"

To the extent possible, reference the ideas throughout therapy sessions. "As you talk about this, how is your nervous system doing?" or "Is this too triggering for your frontal lobes? Are they getting a little overwhelmed?" or "It sounds as if your amygdala really freaks out around people who are very loud—especially men. And then does your thinking brain shut down?" One of the difficulties experienced by trauma survivors is the failure of the traumatized brain to integrate past and present, safe now versus dangerous then, regular feelings versus triggered trauma-related emotions. The more the workbook materials become part of the conversation in psychotherapy, the more easily clients will integrate what they learn.

MANAGING NEGATIVE REACTIONS TO THE FLIP CHART OR WORKBOOK

Invariably, some clients will be triggered by the flip chart, the workbook, or both. Some might see the word *trauma* in a title and immediately feel triggered. Some will associate psychoeducation with negative school experiences of being humiliated as "stupid" or shamed about their "lack of education." Some experience psychoeducation as "being lectured to" or "being in school." Longing for relief and a feeling of unconditional acceptance in therapy, some clients can be irritated by what feels academic instead of caring. Expect that some clients will refuse to use the chart, the book, or both—or be unable to use either because they are too triggered and dysregulated. On the other hand, some clients will find these two tools indispensable: The visual images of the flip chart will enable them to focus even when spacey or overwhelmed, and they are more likely to feel validated by the information and better understood. Survivors of trauma email me constantly to thank me for the flip chart and to tell me how much it means to them. But do not be surprised when other clients ask you to put one or the other away so they do not have to see them!

There is no need to struggle with any client over the use of these tools. It is best to validate clients' negative responses but to ask them to be curious as well: "Wow, so this is really triggering, huh? What gets triggered when I show you the flip chart (or the worksheet)?" or "Thank you for telling me why it is so triggering—I get it now" or "What a shame that it reminds you of school and the torture of having dyslexia back at a time when no one recognized it! It is too bad because the book does help a lot of people—if it is not too triggering."

With some clients, I might tell the story of how Judy Herman discovered the importance of educating trauma survivors to be full collaborators and to ask their opinion about her ideas. With other clients, I may try to offer the same psychoeducation but without the use of the flip chart or the workbook: "Your nervous system really reacted, huh?" or "I bet your thinking brain just shut down—you probably did not have a chance to think before it just went off like a light bulb—that is what happens to trauma survivors." As the therapist, you can still familiarize yourself with the flip chart and workbook and use the same concepts in talking to the client: "Of course, you do not remember many of the events of your childhood, but you remember a lot: the fear of the dark is most likely a memory; the shame must be a memory— and the hopelessness and the feeling of being inferior or at fault. You have a lot of feeling and body memories even if your brain does not remember many events."

Last but not least, when the client is not ready for a particular intervention, the therapist can do what wise parents learn to do: Wait for a more opportune moment or find another way to introduce the same concept. I can put the flip chart or workbook away, then bring it out a few weeks or months later, or I can reference it periodically: "It is a shame the workbook is so triggering..." or "It is too bad that the flip chart reminds you of school and those mean teachers..." or "If I did not know how triggering it is, I would bring out the flip chart right now... but is it okay if I tell you about trauma and the brain?" And if the client says no, then I have to accept that decision. I can be transparent and say, "I would rather you know what is happening inside you so it is not just me that knows, but you are in charge of these decisions about your own treatment, and I can respect that."

USING TRIGGERS AS AN OPPORTUNITY TO PRACTICE THE SKILLS

Some clients will want to use the flip chart and/or workbook but then find themselves triggered by certain words, ideas, diagrams, or worksheets. Or the client may come to sessions chronically triggered or triggered by some specific experience earlier in the day. If either occurs, you have an opportune moment to use the book to help the client manage and learn from the experience of being triggered. A workbook is not a textbook. Finishing it is less important for clients than is gaining practice in using its concepts and skills to help themselves when triggered or flooded. For example, if the client is obviously triggered in a session (e.g., highly anxious, reactive, angry, defensive or spacy, numb, and shut down), Worksheet 6 can be very useful because it focuses on the client's ability to identify being triggered. Worksheet 5 is very appropriate if the client is chronically triggered. As therapist, I might point out, "You [or your body] are really triggered today, huh? Have you been triggered all day? Did you wake up triggered this morning? Or did something trigger you in the course of the morning?" Then I might suggest, "Let us work on a trigger log together—that will help you anticipate a lot of the triggers so they do not catch you by surprise." We can start to fill out the worksheet in the session, and then I can suggest that the client take it home and keep working on it.

Because the ability to recognize triggered responses and to differentiate real and present danger from a triggered sense of threat is so crucial to trauma recovery, time spent on these issues in therapy is always valuable. There is no rush to go on to other chapters and topics if the client's primary challenge is sensitivity to triggers and difficulty managing triggered responses. In trauma recovery, certain issues (and thus certain sections of the flip chart or workbook) may take center stage for months and months, and then other issues and chapters might become relevant—but not necessarily in the same order as a table of contents. Always go where the client's needs and difficulties take you, for better and for worse, and use the book accordingly.

The psychotherapeutic skill of attuning to the client and using your presence to help clients stay present and tolerate their distressing emotions is at the heart of all therapy. Using the workbook in an attuned, flexible, responsive way is key to its success and to its meaning in the client's life. For me as a therapist and author, the client's connection to the book, the felt sense of it as a support or ally in the battle to overcome the traumatic past, is even more important than its completion. I want survivors to feel my presence, as well as yours, urging them on and holding the conviction that they can do it—they can heal. We are on their side.

1

The Living Legacy of Trauma

Once thought to be a rare event, we now know that traumatic experiences happen to millions of human beings every year. Whether the trauma is long-term exposure to a traumatic environment (e.g., child abuse, domestic violence, war) or a single catastrophic event (e.g., terrorist attack or car accident), all human beings are vulnerable to trauma or impacted by the trauma experienced by those they love. What most individuals do not know, however, is that **a traumatic event is not over when it is over**—even if we have successfully survived.

RECOGNIZING THE LIVING LEGACY OF TRAUMA

The effects of trauma often endure for weeks, months, years, even decades afterward. It is a living legacy.

Unlike the feelings we have about relics of the past, such as a grandmother's vase, a father's watch, or a mother's ring, a living legacy is not recognizable as an antique. The living legacy of trauma manifests in intense physical, perceptual, and emotional reactions to everyday things—rarely recognizable as past experience. These emotional and physical responses, called "implicit memories," keep bringing the trauma alive in our bodies and emotions again and again, often many times a day. Reactivated in day-to-day life by apparently harmless reminders related to the original situation or situations, our bodies tense up, our hearts pound, we see horrifying images, and we feel fear, pain, or rage. We startle as if facing Godzilla even in the safety of our own homes, or we feel a sudden wave of painful shame and lose the capacity to speak. We feel loneliness and heartache even when surrounded by people who care about us, or we experience the desperate impulse to run away and hide from them. If past traumatic events occurred in the context of family, home, neighborhood, and close attachment relationships, those arenas will become a land mine field of potential triggers that can be tripped by the simplest daily routines—even waking up, eating breakfast, taking a shower, brushing one's teeth, or going to work or school.

Worse yet, there may be no event or picture to which we can connect these nonverbal memories. Decades of research on the effects of trauma confirm that overwhelming experiences are less likely to be recalled in a clear, coherent narrative or a series of pictures that we can describe. Trauma is more likely to be remembered in the form of sensory elements without words (Ogden, Minton, & Pain, 2006)—emotions, body sensations, changes in breathing or heart rate, tensing, bracing, collapsing, or just feeling overwhelmed. When implicit memories are evoked by triggers or "landmines," we reexperience the sense of threat, danger, humiliation, or impulses to flee that we experienced at the moment of threat—even if we have no conscious verbal memory of what happened.

However, trying to think of a particular event to which these reactions might be connected is unlikely to bring much relief. Often, making the connection to a single event in the past intensifies the painful physical and emotional responses and sense of feeling overwhelmed. Without understanding their meaning, most individuals assume that something is wrong with them or with the current here-and-now environment: "He scared me" or "She shamed me," they conclude, "This is not a safe place." Or they interpret the intense, baffling responses as meaning, "Something is wrong with me" or "I am losing my mind."

Trauma does not just leave behind terrible memories that disrupt the sleep and waking lives of survivors. The living legacy of trauma consists of a gamut of symptoms and difficulties, most of which are unrecognizable as trauma-related, as Figure 1.1 illustrates.

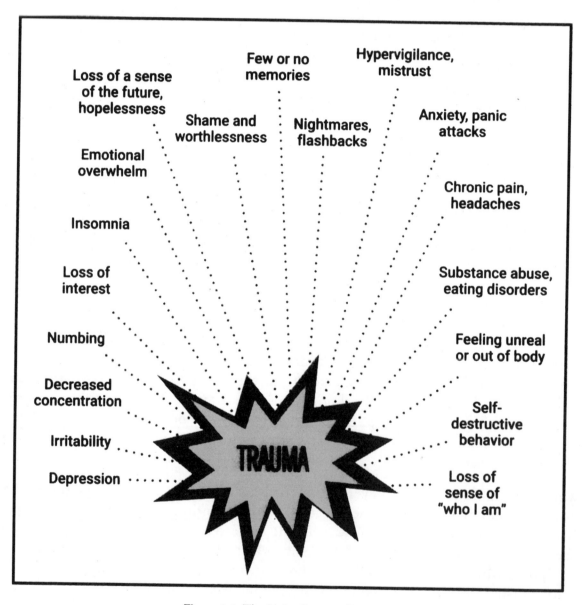

Figure 1.1: The Living Legacy of Trauma

This diagram is meant to remind you and your therapist that a traumatic event is just an event. The living legacy of one overwhelming event or a lifetime of such events is an array of symptoms and difficulties common to individuals who have been traumatized. As you take in all the different effects caused by traumatic experiences, see which ones are most familiar to you. Each represents a way that your mind and body adapted to threat and danger, to being trapped, to being too young or too powerless—or a way that your mind and body adapted to manage all the other feelings and body responses.

> At this point, you can turn to the end of this chapter and use **Worksheet 1: The Living Legacy of Trauma** to explore your own living legacy of trauma. Be curious. If you did not know these symptoms were caused by trauma, what do you think caused them?

Most trauma survivors tend to either blame themselves for their symptoms or blame the immediate environment. They do not experience feelings of relief that "it" is over or any sense of "I made it—I am still alive." Their bodies and emotions still respond to the people and situations around them as if the danger had never ended. When asked, "How long ago was the last traumatic event you experienced?" most trauma survivors are surprised at how much time has gone by because they are still "there," wherever "there" was.

SURVIVING TRAUMA

Why do we not experience trauma as a past event? The answers lie in our brains and bodies.

Human beings do not survive horrific experiences through thoughtful decision making or deliberate planning. In the face of threat, we are too young or too overwhelmed to think and plan. We "make it" because our bodies have the instinct to survive built into them and because we have a brain that prioritizes survival above all else. At the moment our brains perceive a potential life threat, our survival responses are automatically set in motion.

Certain areas of the brain are specialized to help us survive danger (van der Kolk, 2014). A set of related structures in the limbic system hold our capacity for emotional, sensory, and relational experience, as well as the nonverbal memories connected to traumatic events. The limbic system includes the thalamus (a relay station for sensory information), the hippocampus (an area specialized to process memory), and the amygdala (the brain's fire alarm and smoke detector). When our senses pick up the signs of imminent danger, that information is automatically transmitted to the thalamus, where, in a manner of nanoseconds, it is evaluated by threat receptors in the amygdala and in the prefrontal cortex (LeDoux, 2002) to determine if it is a true or false alarm.

The prefrontal cortex, our thinking and perceiving brain, is theoretically designed to hold the "veto power." If the stimulus is recognized as benign, the amygdala is not supposed to respond. But when something might be threatening, the amygdala stimulates the brain to turn on the sympathetic nervous system, initiating an adrenaline stress response that prepares the body to fight or flee. Adrenaline causes an increase in heart rate and respiration, maximizing oxygen flow to our muscles and turning off other non-essential systems, including the prefrontal cortex. We are now in survival mode, where pausing to think might waste precious seconds of response time. But the price we pay for the automatic engagement of our instinctive defenses is a high one. We lose the ability for conscious decision making, and we lose the ability to bear witness to the entirety of the experience. We act and react automatically by crying for help, freezing in fear, fleeing, fighting, or giving in when there is no other way out.

Following a traumatic event, the hippocampus, another tiny structure in the limbic system, is responsible for putting the nonverbal experience into chronological order and perspective preparatory to it becoming a memory that we can put into words. However, the hippocampus is one of the non-essential parts of the mind and body that are suppressed under threat. So, for the very worst of human experiences, the hippocampus is unable to complete its task of memory processing, interfering with our ability to make meaning of what has happened. Having survived the trauma, we are left with an inadequate or fragmented memory record that fails to reflect exactly what has happened and how we endured it.

Some survivors have a clear chronological memory of what happened, but even if they do, they still often lack a sense of having survived it. Worse yet, if the environment is chronically traumatic, as in child abuse and neglect or in domestic violence, an individual's survival response system may become chronically sensitized to anticipate threat, resulting in ongoing physical reactivity to the environment as if it were still dangerous and menacing. Without a clear, coherent verbal memory of what happened, there are only two conclusions that traumatized individuals can draw: either "I am in danger" or "I am defective—something is very wrong with me." Either or both of those conclusions exacerbate the painfulness of having survived only to carry the burden of the living legacy of the trauma for days, weeks, and even years afterward.

> If you have carried the blame or shame for what happened or still live in a state of threat, you might want to turn to the end of this chapter and complete **Worksheet 2: How Did Your Symptoms Help You Survive?** Beginning to understand how these symptoms have helped you survive is the first step to changing your relationship to them.

TRIGGERS AND TRIGGERING

Think back to the days of the cavemen and cavewomen, our forebears. They lived in a very dangerous world, vulnerable to disease, harsh climates, the challenge of providing food for the tribe, and potential attacks by animal and human predators. Survival in that harsh environment was enhanced by the ability to sense danger and to react protectively but also by the ability to keep on going, no matter what happened to their loved ones or themselves. It takes precious seconds or minutes to think about potential danger: "Is it safe to go out looking for food?" or "What are those rustling sounds I hear?" It was most likely advantageous to sense danger rather than having to remember or analyze the level of threat.

Centuries later, human beings still have heightened stress and survival responses. Following experiences of danger, the brain and body become biased to cues indicating potential threat. Cues or stimuli connected even very indirectly to specific traumatic events are called *triggers* and have the potential of evoking strong physical and emotional responses, a phenomenon known as *triggering*. Here is one example:

> *Brianna reported to her therapist that the depression had been much worse in the past two weeks "because the weather has been so cold." Curious, her therapist asked, "What did cold weather mean to you when you were a child?" She recalled, "Where I grew up, cold weather meant snow and ice—it meant we were trapped in the house with my mother. We couldn't go out—there was no way to get away from her. Oh! Is that why I get so depressed in the winter?" Brianna's mother was an abusive alcoholic, and it was not safe for any of the children to be trapped in the house with her. Years later, the coming of winter weather each year triggered hopelessness and depression, the feeling memories connected to Brianna's childhood experience.*

Here is another example:

> *Anita longed for signs that she was important to those in her life, and she was easily hurt when they did not reach out to her—but she was also "spooked" when they did. The failure to invite her or to remember her birthday was triggering, but their invitations or gifts also triggered her. She felt hurt, unimportant, and invisible when her family members were distant, and she felt angry and mistrustful when they reached out. "What do they want from me now?" she would wonder. Her relational life was flooded with emotional memories of being either overlooked or manipulated by her abusive family, feeling memories that prevented her from taking in how much she was loved and valued in her adult life by her family of choice.*

Without a reliable, chronological memory of what happened and tormented by the constant reactivation of nonverbal emotional and body memories, survivors of trauma are apt to find themselves acting and reacting in ways that complicate their situations even more—as we have seen in Figure 1.1. Knowing something about the brain can help them make more sense of their actions and reactions. Let us move on to the next chapter and learn a little bit more about how our brains work.

The Living Legacy of Trauma

Circle those symptoms and difficulties you recognize in yourself or have had in the past. Then put a check mark or asterisk next to those you never knew were the result of your trauma.

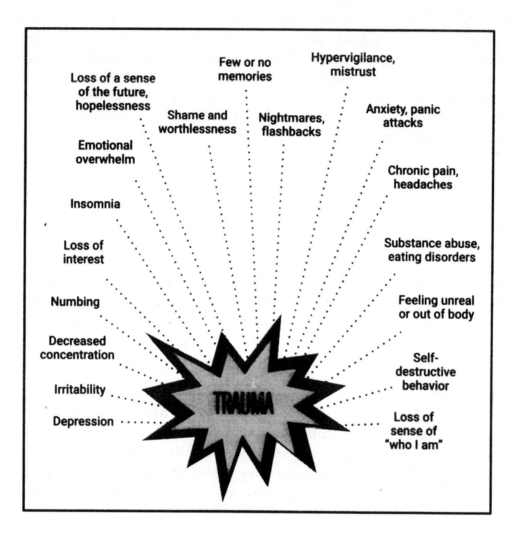

How do your feelings about yourself change when you see that these problems or symptoms are all part of the living legacy of the trauma?

_____

_____

_____

How Did Your Symptoms Help You Survive?

Choose four of your most troubling or difficult trauma symptoms and then ask yourself: "How did the shame help me survive?" "How did the depression help me get through?" "How did losing interest in things help me?" "How did not sleeping help?" "How did using drugs help me survive?" "How did it help to want to die?"

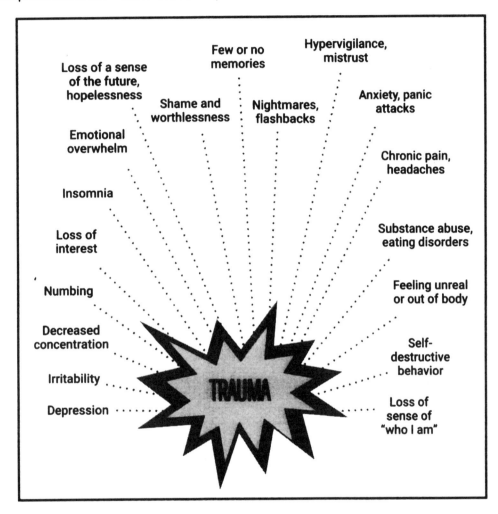

Write in whatever you discover below.

If you are unsure of an answer, just ask yourself, "What would it have been like if I *had not* been depressed [or irritable or ashamed or wanted to die]?"

1. _____

2. _____

3. _____

4. _____

2

Understanding the Traumatized Brain

The brain is the most complex organ in the body, and it affects everything we feel and do, not just what we think. Divided into different structures, each with a different purpose, our brains rely on instantaneous coordination of multiple areas to accomplish most things. If we have lost the car keys, for example, we might try to visualize where we last saw them and then reconstruct, frame by frame, what we did after that. This process requires coordination of two different brain areas: the part of the brain that stores visual memories and the part of the brain in charge of "working memory" (the ability to retrieve past information, compare it to present data, plan, or problem solve). Every day, we rely on the brain to get us through all of our usual routines—but without really understanding how it works.

THE TRIUNE BRAIN MODEL AND THE DEVELOPING BRAIN

The brain model most often used in trauma treatment, called the triune brain, comes from the neuroscientist Paul MacLean (1967) and is now considered out of date by scientists. However, it works for trauma survivors and their therapists because it simplifies the brain into just three areas and therefore is easy to remember and use.

As you can see from Figure 2.1, MacLean divided the brain into three areas: the prefrontal cortex or thinking brain, the animal or mammalian brain, and the reptilian brain. The reptilian brain

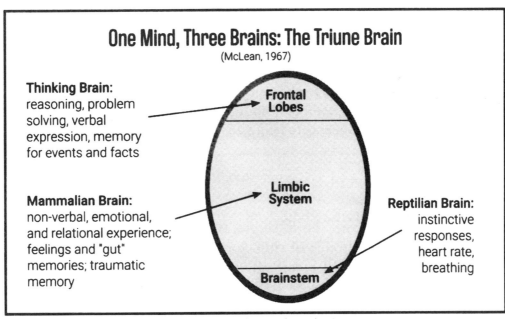

Figure 2.1: Understanding the Brain

is essential to staying alive because it controls basic functions like heart rate and breathing, as well as our reflexes and instinctive responses. Thinking of a lizard makes it easy to see how the reptilian brain works: The lizard does not stop to think—it just responds quickly, automatically, and instinctively. Newborn babies are born with a fairly well-developed reptilian brain and only the beginnings of a mammalian brain and a thinking brain. Their first life challenges are breathing, heart rate, digestion, and regulation of the nervous system. Parents might say, "My baby just sleeps, cries, eats, and poops," not knowing that means the reptilian brain is doing its work of ensuring life.

Then, around three months of age, most babies become more social. They smile when they see a beloved figure appear, wiggle and squeal with excitement, and make little faces and sounds. Their smiles are often so contagious that even weary, sleep-deprived parents cannot help smiling back. This milestone means that the limbic system or mammalian brain is growing rapidly, laying down the foundation for the baby's future emotional and social development. The fact that small children tend to be very emotionally reactive creatures attests to the dominance of the limbic system or mammalian brain during early childhood. Their ability to be rational and organized in their behavioral responses grows very slowly through the childhood years as the thinking brain or prefrontal cortex slowly develops.

By 11 or 12 years of age, most children can use reason instead of emotion to communicate their needs, but, even then, the prefrontal cortex has not yet finished developing. Estimates are that the prefrontal cortex continues to grow and become more elaborated until young people reach the age of approximately 25—in other words, until they are well past the age of adolescence. No wonder adolescents often do not mature until their early 20s! Their brains do not support maturation until the prefrontal cortex has finished its growth and then its reorganization process. If you sometimes feel shame or guilt over how you acted as an adolescent, give the responsibility for your actions to your brain. The rapid growth of the brain at ages 12 to 13 disrupts its maturation. Children suddenly have intense feelings and impulses, as well as a disorganized prefrontal cortex that has suddenly grown bigger but has not yet matured into an organized, wiser brain. Adolescents make decisions based on impulse or emotion, not reason, because their brains have not caught up yet.

> To apply this material to your experience, turn to the end of the chapter to **Worksheet 3: Getting to Know Your Brain,** which will help you identify how each part of your brain contributes to your being you. Be curious. The goal of this worksheet is to help you notice how your brain works.

HOW WE REMEMBER TRAUMA

As we discussed in Chapter One, both single traumatic events and enduring traumatic conditions affect the developing brains of children (Perry et al., 1995). Because danger causes overstimulation of the reptilian and mammalian brains and also shuts down the prefrontal cortex, certain mental processes, such as learning, are often more difficult for traumatized individuals. In children, for example, impulsivity and reactivity can be heightened, leading to a diagnosis of Attention Deficit Hyperactivity Disorder (ADHD) or Oppositional Defiant Disorder, or the child can appear unmotivated. In abusive environments, lower levels of the brain are subject to constant stimulation by threats and/or reminders of past threat and therefore cannot support maturation of the prefrontal cortex.

Neuroscience research has also demonstrated that trauma-related emotional and body memories are stored in the amygdala and are easily activated by triggers or by remembering traumatic events. The research also shows that verbal memory areas (which allow us to tell a story from start to finish) shut down when the amygdala is triggered and reactive. After a traumatic event or a traumatic life, survivors might have only a very fragmented narrative of what happened or no clear story at all. Many survivors say, "I don't remember anything," without realizing that they *are* remembering when they suddenly startle, feel afraid, tighten up, pull back, feel shame or self-hatred, or start to tremble. Because trauma is remembered emotionally and somatically more than it is remembered in a narrative form that can be expressed verbally, survivors often feel confused, overwhelmed, or crazy. Without a memory in words or pictures, they do not recognize what they are feeling as memory.

What they also do not realize is that human beings do not just remember events. We remember in many different ways. As you can see in Figure 2.2, each brain area stores memory in a different way and form. With the thinking brain, we might remember the story of what happened but without a lot of emotion connected to it. With our sensory systems, we might spontaneously see the images or hear the sounds connected to the event. Our emotions might remember how something felt. Our bodies might remember the impulses and movements and the physical sensations (tightening, trembling, sinking feelings, fluttering, quivering) experienced at the time.

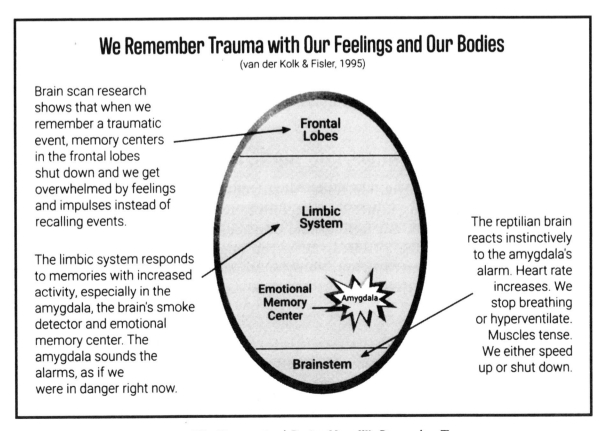

Figure 2.2: The Traumatized Brain: How We Remember Trauma

Most people are unaware of all these different ways of remembering, even though they are all too familiar with the experience of suddenly getting anxious or angry for no apparent reason. When they are triggered, they do not realize that what they are experiencing is a memory. They know the warm feeling that is connected to thinking about loved ones or the pulling back or bracing that occurs when they encounter someone who feels threatening. Many individuals describe *déjà vu* experiences, like "I feel like I've been here before" or "This seems familiar, but I don't know why." Those too are memories without words.

> At this point, you might find it helpful to use **Worksheet 4: How Your Brain Remembers the Trauma** to look at how you might be remembering without words—above and beyond whatever events you recall. Do not focus on memories you can put into words. Instead, be curious about every thought, feeling, or physical reaction that could possibly be a nonverbal memory. One tip to guide you: If the feeling or reaction is painful or confusing or overwhelming, it is likely to be a feeling memory or body memory!

Many trauma survivors feel uncomfortable when they do not remember whole events or when the memories are fragmented or unclear or consist of just a few images, not a whole mental video of the events. Sometimes they doubt themselves and think, "It can't be true because I don't remember exactly what happened" or "I must be making this up or I would remember more clearly." They are expecting to have a clear-cut narrative that can be described in words—like the memory of what they did last weekend.

It is important to know that trauma cannot be remembered the same way other events are recalled because of its effects on the brain. When you feel the impulse to doubt your memory or intuition that something happened to you, remind yourself that recalling events as a story or narrative is not the only way of remembering. You may be remembering a lot more than you think you do!

STARTING TO RECOGNIZE TRIGGERS AND TRIGGERING

Are you surprised at how much you remember when you include distressing feelings, negative thoughts, and physical reactions as memory? Beginning to recognize when we are triggered or when we are remembering with our feelings and our bodies helps all of us to know who and where we are. You might not be a "scaredy-cat"—you might just be experiencing a lot of fear memories. You may not be an "angry person," but you might have feeling memories of anger that get triggered by unfairness or rejection.

> To help you begin to see the relationship between what triggers you and what gets triggered in you—namely, feeling or body memories—start keeping a list each time you might be triggered using **Worksheet 5: Recognizing Triggers and Triggering.** This is a worksheet that many people keep on hand and keep filling out as they unexpectedly encounter triggers in future situations. Remember, you never **choose** to be triggered. It happens to you.

As time goes on, you will start to see patterns. You might notice that certain kinds of things are frequently triggering—for example, authority figures, separation from someone you love, sudden noises, unfairness or rudeness, the dark, or being alone. Assume that whenever you feel overwhelmed, desperate, or numb, something has triggered you. If we assume that what we feel has meaning, even if we do not understand it, we are more likely to see the trigger than if we doubt ourselves or discount what we are feeling as "crazy." Look for very subtle cues that might have triggered what you are feeling. For example, disappointment can be a very huge trigger for trauma survivors, as can being told "No!" or not being understood, having to wait, being ignored or being noticed, or not being believed or taken seriously. Many triggers are paradoxical. Being alone might be a trigger, but being with other people might be also. Change, whether good or bad, is often a trigger, especially if unexpected. As you begin to see patterns of triggers emerging, you will understand more of your story—even when you do not know *why* something is triggering.

Avoid the temptation to connect triggered feelings to specific events in your life. A feeling memory might be the memory of many experiences, not just a single event. Remembering specific events is likely to be even more triggering and therefore increase the intensity. It is more helpful to just acknowledge that you are triggered and to know that being triggered means you are experiencing trauma-related feeling and body memories.

Using the Recognizing Triggers and Triggering Worksheet, you can now start to anticipate triggers: If authority figures are triggering, you can begin to prepare yourself in advance for encountering certain kinds of authority figures. If leaving or having someone leave even for a few hours or days is triggering, you can anticipate the leave-taking and build in some ways to support yourself in the moment. Later chapters will offer you some ideas for how to calm, comfort, energize, or support yourself.

DEALING WITH TRIGGERS AND TRIGGERING

The most difficult aspect about triggering is how it affects our perception of our present lives:

> *Annie felt herself flushing with shame and feeling slightly sick to the stomach each time she drove up to the home she shared with her husband and grown son. If a friend or acquaintance suggested meeting at her house, she would blurt out a hasty "No!" The very thought of someone seeing her home was humiliating to her. She had no idea she was remembering a very different home. Her home as a child was dilapidated and obviously untended, reflecting the chaos inside it. Her alcoholic mother was a respected professional, but the family home revealed dark secrets to anyone passing by. Inside was even worse: unwashed dishes, dirty clothes, and four disheveled children dressed in mismatched, ill-fitting outfits donated by the local church. Thirty years later, the feelings of shame and alarm at the thought of anyone seeing her home persisted as an emotional memory that she assumed was a realistic response to her current home now. She did not see how warm, welcoming, and charming or how carefully kept up it was. Seeing it through the feeling memories led her to conclude, "I have failed—nothing has really changed—I am still 'less than' other people."*

This is a powerful example of why it is crucial for trauma survivors to learn to notice the signs of being triggered. In order to know where we are and who we have become despite the trauma, we have to learn how to discriminate between a here-and-now emotional reaction and a feeling or body memory. To know we or those around us are safe, we have to make those discriminations. Otherwise we will automatically trust those who do not trigger us and distrust all those who do. We will believe the shame is a truth about ourselves rather than understand it as a memory. We will interpret fear as a sign that we are not safe. It took Annie more than 30 years to see her home in present time, to know and feel it was a safe place, and to appreciate how it reflected her journey from trauma to recovery.

> To practice differentiating triggered feelings and perceptions, you might want to fill out **Worksheet 6: How Can You Tell You Are Triggered?** Recognizing the signs of being triggered helps us to know our reality: Am I triggered, or am I really in danger? Am I triggered, or does the shame mean that I am unworthy? Recognizing that we are triggered does not mean that our feelings are unimportant—it means that our feelings are remembering something far worse than what triggers them.

Sometimes, the trigger is something that would bother anyone, such as being startled, yelled at, embarrassed, criticized, ignored, or rejected. All human beings experience some level of distress when such things happen, but if these kinds of events are also triggering, you might experience a "double whammy" effect. Like anyone, you might feel understandably upset and distressed by what has happened but also be triggered by it, multiplying the effect. A feeling of being humiliated might become overwhelming, incapacitating shame if the humiliating event was also triggering.

To make it worse, many traumatized individuals are triggered just by feeling their emotions—any emotion. Because it is usually unsafe for children in traumatic environments to exhibit distress, feeling upset or tearful or angry (or all three combined) can also be triggering.

What is difficult for most trauma survivors is that feeling and body memories do not feel like memories. The shame feels real right now. The fear or terror make us feel unsafe right now. There is nothing that says, "Don't worry—you are just remembering." Bessel van der Kolk, one of the pioneers in the trauma field, reminds therapists that "we must most of all help our patients to live fully and securely in the present" (van der Kolk, 2014, p. 73). It is easy to access the past; all that is needed is a trigger. What is difficult for trauma survivors is to be *here*, now. Think of this step in your recovery as taking on a project to help your body learn that you are *here*, not there. And your brain can help you do that, as you will see in the next chapter.

Getting to Know Your Brain

Write on the diagram what each part of your brain contributes to your everyday life. Perhaps your thinking brain is a resource, or maybe it goes in circles or never turns off. Maybe your emotions are a strength, or maybe they are overwhelming. Maybe your reptilian brain overreacts, or it freezes and cannot allow you to take action when you want to do so.

Write down whatever you notice.

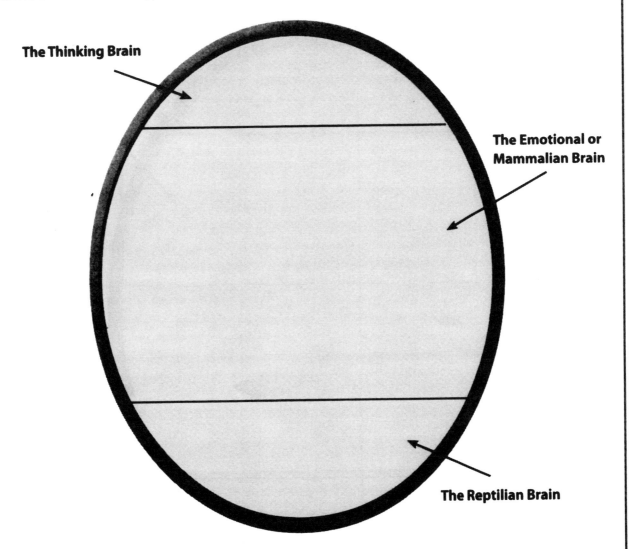

The Thinking Brain

The Emotional or Mammalian Brain

The Reptilian Brain

What parts of your brain are a resource for you?

What parts give you the most difficulty or cause the biggest problems?

The "triune brain" model (McLean, 1967)

How Your Brain Remembers the Trauma

Write in what each part of your brain remembers. **There is no need to write in all the details.** Just a few words or sentences is fine—such as "I remember what happened" or "I don't remember my childhood" or "I can talk about it without any feelings" or "I only have overwhelming feelings and reactions."

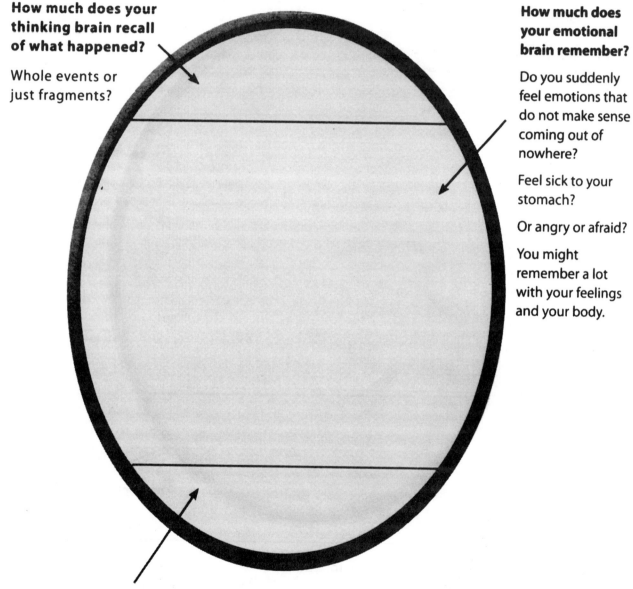

How much does your thinking brain recall of what happened?

Whole events or just fragments?

How much does your emotional brain remember?

Do you suddenly feel emotions that do not make sense coming out of nowhere?

Feel sick to your stomach?

Or angry or afraid?

You might remember a lot with your feelings and your body.

How much does your reptilian brain remember?
Do you startle easily? Pull away from people? Brace for no reason? Go numb?
Does your heart race?

Recognizing Triggers and Triggering

Each time you think you might be triggered, write in your reaction (feelings, thoughts, physical responses), its intensity, what was happening just before, and how you coped. Did you try to ignore it or suppress it? Did you judge yourself or the trigger? Do not judge, just notice.

Date, time, situation	Feelings, thoughts, and physical sensations that got triggered	Intensity: 0–10	Trigger: What was happening just before?	Coping: What did you do to cope?

How Can You Tell You Are Triggered?

Recognizing the signs of being triggered helps us to know our reality: Am I triggered, or am I really in danger? Do I need to leave my job, or am I just experiencing being triggered? Recognizing that we are triggered does not mean our feelings are unimportant. It means that our feelings are remembering something far worse than what triggers them.

Check the signs of being triggered that you recognize:

☐ **Shaking, quivering**	☐ **Wanting to run away**
☐ **Overwhelming emotions**	☐ **Teeth clenching**
☐ **Difficulty breathing**	☐ **Feels unbearable**
☐ **Body wants to collapse**	☐ **Terrified, panicky**
☐ **Feeling "possessed"**	☐ **Hating myself**
☐ **Wanting to give up or die**	☐ **Hating others**
☐ **Wanting to hurt myself**	☐ **Feeling rage**
☐ **Wanting to drink or use drugs**	☐ **Feeling overwhelming shame**
☐ **Knees knocking**	☐ **Emotions do not fit the situation**
☐ **Going numb all over**	☐ **Actions do not fit the situation**
☐ **Sudden intense physical or emotional reactions**	☐ **Clenching or churning or pit in stomach**

When you recognize the signs of being triggered, just keep reminding yourself that "it's just triggering—I am triggered—that's all that is happening."

3

How the Brain Helps Us Survive

Some unexpected and unnoticed trigger evokes alarm, and our bodies suddenly brace or startle. Our hearts begin to pound. Simultaneously, the thinking brain or prefrontal cortex goes offline, making it difficult to think but easier to respond quickly and instinctively if we really are in danger. Without a thinking brain, we cannot step back and assess the situation or ponder the best alternative. There is no time to think in an emergency situation. Instinct is always better and faster when immediate survival is at stake, but once the threat is over, we need mindful awareness and the ability to think in order to heal from the traumatic past.

That, however, is made difficult by the fact that the brain and body continue to respond to everyday life as if we were in danger. Years later, even when our worlds are safe, the same emergency responses are activated whenever some trigger sets off this internal alarm system. When such experiences happen daily, trauma survivors feel overwhelmed and confused. They wonder, "Why am I so angry? So fearful? So ashamed?" And the most common conclusions they reach are either "There is something wrong with me," which makes them feel more ashamed, fearful of being found out, or defensive, or "There is something wrong with my home/job/ friends/partner/way of life," which usually increases anxiety, anger, shame, or hopelessness. And the worse we feel, of course, the more impulsive we become.

The triggers, as well as the automatic conclusions we reach, deactivate the thinking brain, leaving the reptilian brain free to act on instinct. And what does the reptilian brain instinctively seek? Relief and a sense of safety. The desperate impulse to find quick relief, coupled with the loss of ability to judge the consequences of our behavior, invariably exposes individuals to further danger or becomes an increasingly vicious circle.

No one is to blame. The brain and body are simply responding to perceived threat. We do not consciously *choose* to lose our ability to think and plan—it is automatic.

HEALING AND THE THINKING BRAIN

The thinking brain does more for us, however, than simply allowing us to think clearly and make good decisions. To heal—to feel safe now and to know we are safe—requires restoring activity to the prefrontal cortex so that we can observe, reflect, see ourselves and others in perspective, and have access to curiosity and compassion. Wisdom requires this part of the brain. When we use the expression *wise mind*, we are actually referring to the medial prefrontal cortex, located right behind the middle of the forehead. Its job is to help us observe the environment, ourselves, and those around us, to literally see the big picture. We use that part of the brain when we meditate, notice, or focus on something specific, and mentally sit back and look at things from a distance. It also helps us to integrate information from other parts of the brain. We might think, "I'm nervous," and then notice that our knees are trembling and hearts beating faster.

Most of all, the medial prefrontal cortex or wise mind has a calming effect on the amygdala, the structure believed to be an emotional memory center where trauma-related feeling and body memories are stored or encoded. The amygdala also serves a sentry function, scanning the environment for potential threats. When we activate our wise minds, we send a signal to the body and the nervous system that it is safe here now, and the amygdala automatically decreases its activity. Think of it like the smoke detector in your home that is usually set off when the toast is burning: When we activate the medial prefrontal cortex, we can discriminate better, and when we recognize the smell as the toast burning, the brain's smoke detector stops beeping.

If you take a look at Figure 3.1, you will see how the thinking brain can help you to change automatic traumatic responses. Even though we cannot reason with the reptilian brain or with our emotions, we can use the thinking brain to help calm the body and the nervous system by taking advantage of its ability to observe and to differentiate the past from the present.

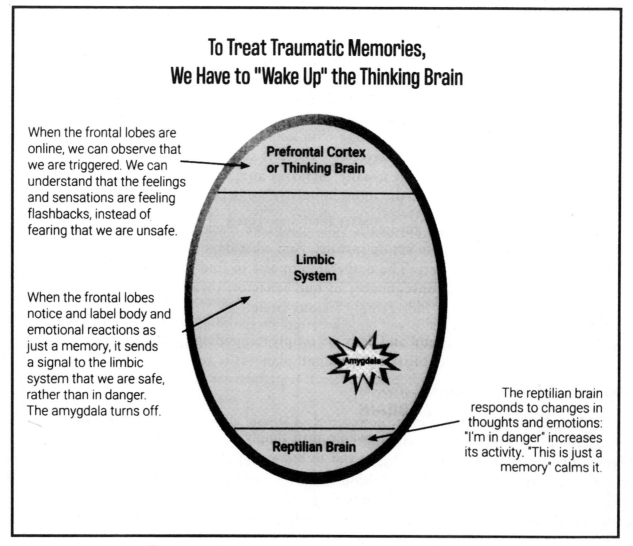

Figure 3.1: Using Our Brains to Heal the Effects of Trauma

HOW DO WE KNOW WHEN A TRAUMATIC EVENT IS OVER?

In a traumatic situation, things happen quickly and are overwhelming in their intensity. When the thinking brain shuts down, we cannot make any sense of what is happening—and that is why most survivors lack the felt awareness that the event has finally ended. It is done and over, but it does not feel finished. The only way to know that we are safe is either to feel relief and a physical sense of safety in the body *or* to assess intellectually whether we are safe or still in danger. But if the brain's internal alarm system is activated and responding as if the threat exists now, we will continue to feel unsafe.

You can easily see how this system helped primitive man and woman survive: having a brain and body biased in favor of perceiving threat meant over-responding to danger, not under-responding. As you learned in Chapter One, the cavemen and cavewomen who under-responded to the myriad threats facing them were less likely to survive, and those who over-responded were more likely to be on the alert and ready to defend. The brain's negativity bias (Hanson, 2013) keeps us on guard against danger, but its effects haunt survivors of trauma for years and even decades after the events have ended.

Perhaps because it was not adaptive in the days of primitive man to relax into a sense of safety, the body's emergency stress response only knows how to go to extremes. It has just two speeds: "Don't just sit there—*do* something!" and "Don't move—it's not safe." Each one is driven by a different branch of the autonomic nervous system, the brain system that controls our emotions, physical reactions, and impulses. Both branches of the nervous system are specialized to respond differently, giving us more options for survival.

When we are in danger, as you will see in Figure 3.2, first, the sympathetic nervous system is immediately mobilized. Heart rate speeds up to increase oxygen flow to muscle tissue. We feel

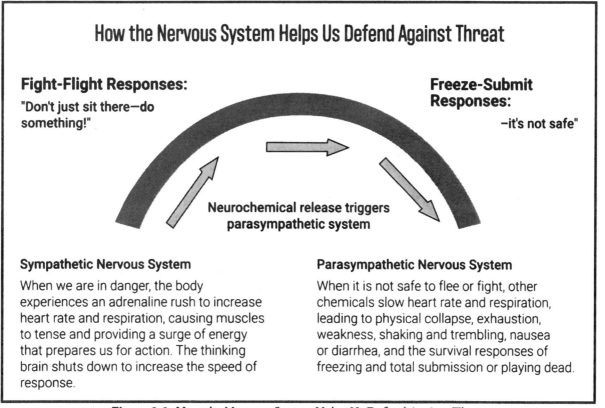

Figure 3.2: How the Nervous System Helps Us Defend Against Threat

a surge of energy, and all non-essential systems in the body shut down, including the thinking brain, so that all our energy is focused on fighting, fleeing, ducking, or getting out of sight.

Two conditions then activate the parasympathetic system. If defending ourselves is more dangerous than complying, or if we are trapped, the parasympathetic nervous system acts as a brake on our defensive impulses, and we become passive and compliant. We "play dead." If we survive the danger and the threat is over, then the parasympathetic system helps us rest, lick our wounds, and repair.

> You can use **Worksheet 7: Differentiating Past and Present** to help you notice whether your mind and body are in the past or if they are in the present. Experiencing a past moment in the here and now feels unpleasant but not unsafe once we know we are remembering rather than in danger.

Children, for example, are almost entirely dependent on freezing and "playing dead" responses, as are battered wives, prisoners of war, and hostages. It is not safe for the less powerful to flee or fight—it would simply increase the risk of harm—and the human body and brain are organized to instinctively choose the most adaptive survival response in the moment.

Perhaps you have wondered, "Why didn't I fight back?" The answer is that "you" did not make that decision. Your body and brain determined that it was not safe to fight. Your thinking brain turned off, and your body instinctively decided what to do next.

> Use **Worksheet 8: How Our Nervous System Defends Us** to observe how your nervous system works. Whatever you notice will not just help you understand your actions and reactions now. These patterns will also help to tell you more about how you survived.

HOW POST-TRAUMATIC SYMPTOMS REFLECT OUR TRAUMA HISTORY

The ingredients of post-traumatic stress disorder (PTSD) are found in the ways our nervous system still keeps trying to save our lives long after the danger is over. When we are triggered, high sympathetic activation communicates an alarm to the body and mind: "Red alert! Watch out for danger!" It provides a surge of physical energy, strong instinctive impulses, and the icy calm that gives us a sense of superhuman power. But if action was dangerous then, the body may have come to perceive sympathetic arousal as a threat, automatically triggering the parasympathetic system to slam on the brakes, bringing our movements to a grinding halt. Years later, the parasympathetic system may still be dominant, robbing individuals of energy, drive, and confidence.

Not knowing that their brains and bodies are causing these feelings and reactions, not knowing that traumatic events have conditioned their nervous systems to react in these ways, trauma survivors blame themselves and think, "I'm depressed—even though I have nothing to be depressed about" or "I'm just an angry person" or "I don't know why I'm afraid of everything—I'm just a chicken." But blaming ourselves is triggering, and it can also propel many individuals to try to fix these problems in ways that further worsen the situation. We have a nervous system adapted to threat even if we now live in a world that is rarely dangerous, and that adaptation keeps the living legacy of trauma actively mobilized in our bodies even when we do not need it anymore.

Figure 3.3 depicts the most common patterns of autonomic activation that develop as a response to chronic or repeated threat. As you look at the diagram, notice which patterns of arousal are most familiar to you. The pattern of nervous system responses to the environment and to ordinary stress that you notice in your life today tells the story of your survival, reflecting how it adapted to the traumatic conditions you once faced. Did you survive by being constantly on guard, tense, fearful, and reactive? Or did you survive by shutting down, going numb, and spacing out? Was it better for you to run or fight? Or was it better to collapse and go passive? Your body is actually telling you what was safest then, even if it is not helpful now. This diagram can also serve as a way to notice when you are outside of the window of tolerance and as a reminder to slow down or speed up.

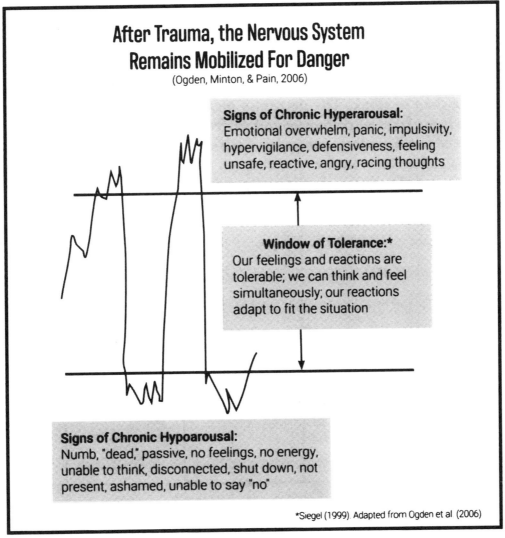

Figure 3.3: A Nervous System Adapted to a Dangerous and Threatening World

Worksheet 9: Trauma and the Window of Tolerance can help you become aware of how your sympathetic and parasympathetic nervous systems still react after the trauma has passed, how they still affect your feelings and behavior, and how much you may need a wider window of tolerance. Often, our sympathetic and parasympathetic responses occur predictably. Certain situations trigger one response or the other, and certain situations are positive triggers that help widen the window of tolerance. Include that information on the worksheet, too, to help yourself anticipate trauma-related triggers and seek out positive triggers.

Remember you had no control over how your nervous system responded at the time. The brain reacts long before we have conscious awareness of the situation, and we cannot control our instinctive reactions any more than a lizard can. Increasing awareness of these reactions as nervous system memories or survival responses often helps them to feel more tolerable. When we do not understand why we are going numb or jumping out of our skins, we feel more alarmed and ashamed of our reactions.

Without awareness of why they are having these reactions, desperate to stop them from happening, and unable to think clearly, many survivors of trauma find themselves acting impulsively. Caring about the consequences of our actions requires a thinking brain and some sense of having the time to think. The desperate measures to which trauma survivors resort when triggered can range from workaholism and perfectionism to over-use of food and alcohol to severe substance abuse disorders, compulsive self-harm, life-threatening eating disorders, or suicidal impulses and actions. In the next chapter, we will examine how to understand and work with these patterns of behavior that initially induce feelings of greater safety in the body but eventually become a threat to life and stability.

Differentiating Past and Present

Learning to recognize when we are reacting to the past helps us to know when we are safe (but triggered) *versus* when we are in real danger. It helps us to feel less hopeless, less afraid, less angry, less depressed, and less crazy. It helps to know when we are remembering. Any time you feel distress, study what is going on by filling out this worksheet.

Time of day	What are you doing?	What feelings and sensations are you aware of?	What belief seems to explain why you are feeling this way?	Do these thoughts/ feelings make more sense in the present or in the past?

What happens when you identify a feeling as making more sense in the past than now?

How Our Nervous System Defends Us

Describe how your nervous system works. When you get triggered, what does your sympathetic nervous system do? What are your fight-or-flight responses like? What does your parasympathetic system do? Which is more familiar?

Fight-Flight Responses:

Freeze-Submit Responses:

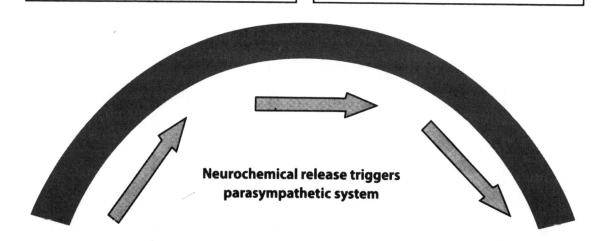

Neurochemical release triggers parasympathetic system

Sympathetic Nervous System:

Parasympathetic Nervous System:

Trauma and the Window of Tolerance

Circle the signs of autonomic hyper- and hypoarousal that you notice in yourself, and add any other signs not listed here. Write in the situations that seem to stimulate these different states. For example, are you more hyperaroused when alone or when around people? Are you more in the window of tolerance at work?

Signs of Chronic Hyperarousal:

Emotional overwhelm, panic, impulsivity, hypervigilance, defensiveness, feeling unsafe, reactive, angry, racing thoughts, AND:

_____

_____

_____

When do I find myself hyperaroused?

_____

_____

_____

Window of Tolerance:

My feelings and reactions are tolerable; I can think and feel simultaneously; My reactions adapt to fit the situation; AND:

_____

_____

_____

When do I find myself in the window of tolerance?

_____

_____

_____

Signs of Chronic Hypoarousal:

Numb, "dead," passive, no feelings, no energy, unable to think, disconnected, shut down, not present, ashamed, unable to say "no," AND:

_____

_____

_____

When do I find myself hypoaroused?

_____

_____

_____

4

The Challenge of Post-Traumatic Coping

In a threatening world, with no support, protection, or comfort, children have to rely upon the limited resources of their own bodies to manage overwhelming circumstances and unbearable feelings. Infants have the fewest resources because the body and nervous system are still immature at birth, yet even a baby can dissociate or go into a limp, numb parasympathetic state. Toddlers and preschoolers have a few more options. They can use food to soothe themselves and masturbate to stimulate pleasurable feelings. They can also stimulate adrenaline production through hyperactive or risky behavior. As children reach latency and early puberty, even more options become available: They can restrict food, binge and purge, develop obsessive-compulsive patterns of behavior, act out sexually, pinch or scratch themselves, and even fantasize about suicide. Less self-destructive coping can also develop: getting lost in books or fantasy, parentified behavior, or over-achievement.

In adolescence, the growing physical strength and capability of the body facilitates a new array of options for self-regulation. Running away is now a choice. Teenagers also have greater access to cigarettes and drugs, or they can act out sexually, engage in more severe eating-disordered behavior, and have the strength to act on suicidal impulses. The physical body is now capable of violence, whether aggressive behavior toward others or self-inflicted violence, unchecked by an inhibited or immature prefrontal cortex. As the saying goes, "Desperate times call for desperate measures," and often desperate self-destructive measures are a well-conditioned pattern of response by the time traumatized children reach adulthood. Ask yourself, "How old was I when I first started to _____ as a way to manage my feelings?"

DESPERATE EFFORTS TO REGULATE A TRAUMATIZED NERVOUS SYSTEM

Every type of addictive, eating-disordered, and self-destructive behavior produces a neurochemical reaction in the human body. Let us take a closer look at some of the common ways in which trauma survivors attempt to regulate their trauma responses.

Self-injury (cutting, head banging, punching walls, or even hitting ourselves) brings quick relief to the body by stimulating the production of adrenaline and endorphins, two neurochemicals that decrease pain. As discussed in the previous chapter, adrenaline produces a surge of energy and a physical sense of strength, and it also induces a state best described as "calm, cool, and collected." Doctors, nurses, and EMTs all rely on adrenaline to do their jobs well, as do most peak performers. Endorphins are the neurochemicals associated with relaxation, pleasure, and pain relief; they are the body's "happy" chemicals. The combination of these two chemical responses triggered by self-harm is responsible for the very immediate and complete physical and emotional relief felt by those who self-injure.

Restricting food intake puts the body into a neurochemical state called ketosis, creating a numbing effect but also a boost of increased energy. No wonder individuals with anorexia can eat so little and still work out at the gym for hours. Binging and overeating, on the other hand, both have a numbing and relaxing effect.

Drugs (whether illicit substances or prescription drugs) cause many different effects, from sedation and numbing to stimulation and increased feelings of power and control. Alcohol is a mild stimulant in small doses and a relaxant in larger doses, bringing some relief to trauma survivors who experience both anxiety and depression. Marijuana serves the purpose of inducing a steady state of hypoarousal and numbing, especially when taken at intervals throughout the day.

Compulsive hyperactivity, workaholism, and high-risk behavior of all kinds also tend to stimulate adrenaline production, whereas retreating to one's bed and curtailing activity tends to increase feelings of spaciness and numbing.

Long before substance use becomes abuse or self-harm becomes active suicidality, trauma survivors initially learn that they can successfully control their symptoms and function in the world by using their drugs and behaviors of choice. I use the term *successfully* because, to the extent that substance use, eating disorders, or self-harm bring symptom relief to the survivor, it may prevent suicidality, loss of functioning, social withdrawal, and a host of other problems common to those who have been traumatized.

Figure 4.1 illustrates the ways in which people instinctively try to cope with their hyper- or hypoarousal in order to get relief. These behaviors provide a temporary false window of tolerance, offering a sense of "I can handle this" that is time-limited and illusory.

What Happens When There Is Only a Very Narrow Window Of Tolerance?

Chronic Hyperarousal:
Overwhelmed by intense emotions, physical reactions, and self-destructive impulses, individuals seek immediate relief by drinking, using drugs, self-harming, not eating (or eating too much), binging and purging, and even planning suicide—anything that decreases the hyperactivation and provides a false sense of having a window of tolerance.

Narrow Window of Tolerance:*
Even a little bit of emotion or activation feels intolerable.

Chronic Hypoarousal:
Feeling numb, dead, or empty inside, individuals resort to stimulants, self-harm, or binging and purging to increase activation. Or they seek to sustain feelings of numbness through the daily use of marijuana and other downers. They too are reassured by the false sense of having a window of tolerance.

*Siegel (1999) Adapted from Ogden et al. (2006)

Figure 4.1: How Trauma Survivors Cope with Traumatized Nervous System

Turn to **Worksheet 10: How Do You Try to Regulate Your Traumatized Nervous System?** to explore how you have learned to regulate yourself. How do you try to manage your nervous system and distressing emotions? What is your "go-to" way of feeling better? Your second most familiar way of trying to manage traumatic activation? Do not judge yourself—just be curious about how these behaviors help! Whatever you notice will not only help you understand your actions and reactions as ways you are trying to help yourself, but it will also tell you more about how you survived. Was survival dependent upon staying frightened and on guard? Ashamed and people-pleasing? Or shut down and numb? Or being constantly on the run?

THE VICIOUS CIRCLE OF ADDICTIVE AND SELF-DESTRUCTIVE BEHAVIOR

Any addictive or self-destructive behavior begins as a survival strategy: as a way to numb, wall off intrusive memories, self-soothe, increase hypervigilance, combat depression, or facilitate dissociating. But compulsive behaviors also have a "drug effect" that wears off after a few minutes or hours, increasing the sense of need or urgency to repeat the action or substance to prevent losing that positive effect. With repeated use, the body develops tolerance, meaning that these psychoactive substances (whether alcohol, heroin, or the body's own chemicals like adrenaline) require continual increases in dosage to maintain the original degree of relief and eventually are needed just to ward off physical and emotional withdrawal effects.

Were it not for the body's increasing tolerance, trauma survivors could use these means of obtaining relief in a moderate, low-risk way for years. Instead, over time, eating disorders become increasingly worse, substance use becomes abuse, self-harm becomes more dangerous, and suicidal thoughts and wishes become more actively life-threatening. Thus, the substance use or self-destructive behavior may begin as an effective approach to managing post-traumatic reactions, but then it gradually acquires a life of its own, becoming increasingly disruptive to the survivor's functioning until it is a greater threat than the symptoms it attempts to keep at bay.

Once the thinking brain matures in our 20s, we have more capacity to appreciate the consequences of unsafe behavior and more ability to think before we act, but that increased awareness often results in shame: "Why am I doing this? If anyone knew, they would judge me. I need to stop, but I can't!" Survivors may hate themselves for using these ways of coping, but the alternative is worse. The emotions and implicit memories that were dangerous to feel or acknowledge long ago still trigger the same sense of threat—and the same desperate need to stop them at all cost.

Without understanding the method to their madness, the logical conclusion most trauma survivors reach is: "There must be something wrong with me—I must be defective." Their shame and self-blame of course trigger more intense, intolerable feelings—further increasing the need to do something to make the feelings stop. They are now literally, as the saying goes, "between a rock and a hard place." If they stop the behaviors that stem the tide of overwhelming feelings, then the feelings will be even more intolerable. If they do not stop, the shame worsens into self-hatred. Few trauma survivors realize that their self-destructive behavior represents an ingenious attempt to regulate their nervous systems and their unbearable physical and emotional reactions.

When you are a trauma survivor who has learned to manage overwhelming feelings using addictive, eating-disordered, or unsafe behavior, it takes more than this book alone to address both the trauma and the ways you are coping with it. This way of thinking about how you have learned to survive and adapt, however, is an important first step. In the next chapter, we address how to observe and begin to change high-risk patterns for managing traumatic responses.

How Do You Try to Regulate
Your Traumatized Nervous System?

Hyperarousal

How do you try to regulate your hyperarousal? Without judging yourself, list all the things you do to bring your activation down or to stop emotions from becoming overwhelming.

_____

_____

_____

_____

_____

_____

Narrow Window of Tolerance:*
Even a little bit of emotion feels intolerable

Hypoarousal

How do you try to regulate your hypoarousal? Does it regulate you, or do you regulate it? Without judging yourself, list all the ways you try to bring your activation up or keep yourself numb and detached.

_____

_____

_____

_____

_____

_____

*Siegel (1999)

5

Recovering from Self-Destructive Patterns of Coping

Willpower never works when the prefrontal cortex or thinking brain is shut down. Worse yet, safety, sobriety, or abstinence may initially result in increased hyper- or hypoarousal and a shutting down of the prefrontal cortex. Treatment programs are often essential for stabilization of eating disorders, addictions, or suicidality and self-harm, but long-term change in these patterns is impossible in just a few weeks or even months. Traditional psychiatric hospitalizations for unsafe behavior contain the risk of harm but rarely offer trauma treatment or result in helping survivors develop new, more adaptive coping patterns. As necessary as these programs are when individuals are at risk, a longer-term approach is needed beyond the hospital or treatment center.

AN INTEGRATED MODEL FOR TREATING TRAUMA AND ADDICTIVE BEHAVIOR

The mental health world has always been divided, treating substance abuse as a public health or medical issue and treating trauma, eating disorders, and suicidality as psychiatric disorders. The tendency toward specialization can make it even more difficult to find help for both. Many trauma survivors complain that eating disorder professionals do not understand the role of the trauma in driving their symptoms; those who are suicidal or self-harming feel misunderstood when their trauma histories are ignored or, worse yet, when they are treated as attention seeking and manipulative. The addictions recovery world is increasingly aware of the role of trauma in addictive disorders but still tends to prefer a "treat the addiction first" approach. I would agree that severe addictive and eating disorders do need to be brought under control first so that you can begin to recover the use of your thinking brain. Without it, long-term recovery from either the trauma or the addictive disorder is not possible. However, when professionals acknowledge the survivor's traumatic past and help them to see how the trauma and compulsive behavior complicate each other, it is often easier to engage in the recovery program.

Treatment programs for eating disorders or substance abuse are especially effective when the survivor is participating in them on a daily basis because they stimulate the thinking brain by providing education and structure. In addictions programs, the newly sober individual is challenged to face the phobia of emotion and to develop new ways of coping. However, once outside of these programs, it is much harder to anticipate triggering and regulate what is triggered—which accounts for the high rate of relapse among trauma survivors who graduate from addiction or eating disorder programs. It is not surprising that many trauma survivors find themselves cycling in and out of hospitals and addiction/eating disorder programs without long-lasting benefit, increasing their sense of shame and defectiveness. Even though 12-Step programs—such as Alcoholics Anonymous, Narcotics Anonymous, Overeaters Anonymous, or Sex Addicts and Sex and Love Addicts Anonymous—can be very triggering, their benefits can far outweigh their side effects and I highly recommend them.

In addition, I also recommend that survivors try to find a therapist who understands the complex relationship between trauma and suicidality, trauma and addiction, trauma and eating disorders, or trauma and other kinds of compulsive behavior. The job of the therapist is to remember to look for the adaptive intent and to reframe the disorder or addiction as a valiant attempt to manage overwhelming feelings and memories. Understanding that the individual was desperate and overwhelmed and that these behaviors, in small doses, initially worked is crucial for recovery.

Understanding this process becomes even more crucial when individuals stop using substances or harming the body and begin to experience a profound sense of shame about how self-destructive they have been. But remember that shame and self-blame shut down the prefrontal cortex and diminish the capacity to learn. Curiosity, instead, increases activity in the thinking brain and therefore promotes new learning. So, start by being curious and ask yourself:

- How did _____ (e.g., the drug use, cutting, eating disorder) help me to cope at the time it started? What was different as a result?
- Given that I did not know why I was doing these things, how did I respond when life challenged me to cope more or to cope differently?
- Did I have to use substances, cut, or binge and purge more often? Or did I change my substances of choice? Or did I find new ways to manage my nervous system and my feelings?
- Did I begin to act out in other ways when under the influence (e.g., by engaging in compulsive sexual behavior or being preoccupied with suicide)?
- When did the addiction begin to negatively affect my ability to cope?
- What did I do then?

You may believe that the anorexia helped because it resulted in weight loss or that the cutting worked because you wanted to punish yourself. However, the physiological results of these behaviors do not support such beliefs. Restricting food intake and self-harm both work because they induce numbing and a positive change in bodily state, and that is what we have to be curious about. At each step of the way, it is important to validate that every choice of behavior is and was an attempt you made to stay in control of these powerful forces inside you, even if the attempts were not entirely successful and even if the end result is not a pretty sight. Then, it makes sense that for sobriety and stability to feel safe, individuals must learn new ways of feeling a sense of control—through the acquisition of the skills and inner resources necessary to expand the window of tolerance.

What is different about developing and expanding a resilient window of tolerance versus creating a "false" window of tolerance is that self-destructive and addictive behavior provides immediate relief. Expanding the window of tolerance without self-harm or addictive behavior requires practice—it is anything but immediate! On the other hand, the immediate relief is usually long gone by the time these issues become a family or therapeutic concern. Immediate relief may have occurred when the individual first discovered these ways of controlling the symptoms and emotions. But as he or she continues to cut, restrict, drink, or attempt suicide, relief becomes more and more difficult to achieve as the addiction progresses. Worse yet, the self-destructive, addictive, or eating-disordered behavior gets increasingly dangerous.

THE ABSTINENCE/RELAPSE CYCLE

Once trauma survivors fully grasp the contribution of the addiction or self-destructive behavior at different points in their lives, the next most important idea they need to know about is the Abstinence/Relapse Cycle (Fisher, 1999). As the diagram in Figure 5.1 describes, sobriety or abstinence in the context of trauma can precipitate a whole series of new crises and symptoms because the individual is now totally without the neurochemical barrier and false window of tolerance created by the substance use, eating-disordered behavior, suicidality, or self-injury. What happens to most trauma survivors very early and repeatedly is that, each time they achieve safety, the PTSD symptoms tend to worsen within a matter of weeks, months, or even days, becoming more intrusive and intense.

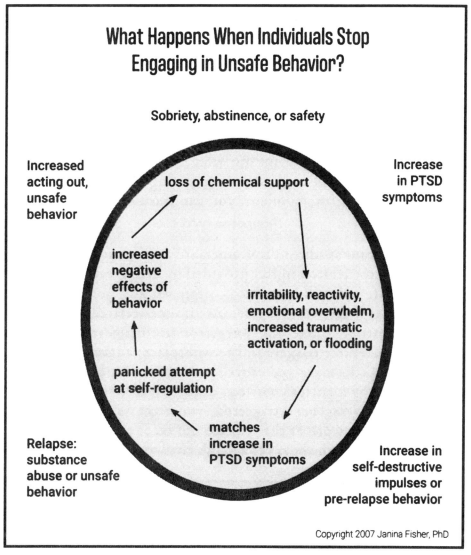

Figure 5.1: The Abstinence/Relapse Cycle

If the symptoms worsened in recognizable ways, that might be easier. Although some survivors start to experience flashbacks and nightmares that validate their traumatic experience, more often what comes up for the newly safe or newly sober individual is a deluge of implicit memories that create overwhelming feelings of irritability, anxiety, reactivity, and vulnerability. Not knowing why they feel these things (and disappointed or frustrated that they do not feel better, as they have been told they would), the addictive craving and self-destructive impulses increase—not always in recognizable ways either. Some individuals might feel resentment or entitlement to drink or hurt themselves; others might feel a desperate sense of needing to do *something*, anything, to stop the feelings. Relapses (in self-harming, eating disorders or addictions) frequently occur as acts of desperation to stem the tide of overwhelm. As one trauma survivor told me to explain the degree of her desperation, "Why do therapists keep asking me to sit with my feelings? They don't understand. I don't have feelings, I have tsunamis!"

> **Worksheet 11: Tracking Your Abstinence/Relapse Cycle** can be very helpful if you find yourself in these dilemmas. Try to avoid the tendency to shame and self-blame and instead be curious about how impulses to stop overwhelming or distressing feelings can lead you back to less healthy ways of coping despite your best efforts.

Using the Abstinence/Relapse Cycle diagram, it is usually easy for most people to see where they are in the cycle: "I'm definitely feeling overwhelmed and irritable, so I guess I'm at the 'increased PTSD symptoms' stage—and pretty soon I'll be hoarding razor blades... tempting but maybe not a good idea" or "I'm starting to feel more resentful and burdened by everyone and everything. I feel like I deserve a drink for what I'm putting up with." Or "I can't stand how big I am—I'm as big as a house—I can't keep eating all this food they tell me to eat." Wherever you are in the cycle at the moment, you can learn to track the signs that anticipate what is likely to happen next.

Once you are safe, sober, or abstinent, it is crucial to anticipate an increase in trauma-related responses. Without the neurochemical buffer provided by drugs, eating disorders, or self-harm, you will find yourself more vulnerable to being triggered and more reactive and emotional. The trauma symptoms complicate recovery because trauma-related triggers tend to reactivate impulses to self-harm, restrict, binge and purge, or use drugs very quickly. For example, many trauma survivors encounter triggers in the workplace: authority figures, arbitrary rules and regulations, pressure to do more and more, low salaries for long hours, and competitive colleagues. Being triggered by a critical boss can quickly lead to the triggering of addictive or self-destructive impulses. Having been triggered, you might skip lunch to induce numbing (rationalizing that you need to work or that you do not want to be seen). Or you might give in to the temptation to go out with the boys for a drink after work to manage the anger or anxiety.

> In the meantime, you can use **Worksheet 12: Breaking the Cycle** to become more aware of these patterns in your life and to practice new alternatives for interrupting and changing them.

The key principle guiding most addiction and psychiatric recovery models is learning to ask for help. However, relying on others is very triggering for most trauma survivors since being vulnerable was so dangerous in a neglectful, abusive world. Even Alcoholics Anonymous and other 12-Step programs can be highly triggering, leading either to avoidance or to impulses to relapse. A trauma therapist can work with you to help you manage the triggered reactions stimulated by learning to ask for help and can assist you in expanding your window of tolerance. However, the good news is that the first and most accessible source of help can be found in your own brain!

GETTING HELP FROM THE "NOTICING BRAIN"

Thinking and noticing are very different ways of relating to the world. We might think, "I really should finish this project today" without noticing that, before the thought is even complete, our bodies feel tired and heavy. We might think, "I shouldn't have done that—I put my foot right in my mouth," not noticing that the self-blame evokes shame and the impulse not to think about it. We might be so preoccupied with anxiety about something that happened yesterday or something that might happen tomorrow that our senses do not register something positive (a flower, the sun, a puppy, someone's smile). The capacity of the human mind to remember the past in chronological detail or to envision a future that is not here yet is both a blessing and a curse. Our thinking brain can spend weeks and months worrying about the past or dreading the future—distracting us from moment-to-moment experiences in our lives that are safe or even satisfying.

The left hemisphere of the brain is in charge of thinking sequentially and in words; the right hemisphere is intuitive and reacts nonverbally. Both of these functions are important. We have to be able to think and plan, learn from experience, link cause and effect, and anticipate how to deal with the future. And we have to be able to sense our gut reactions and our intuition when logic is not enough. Trauma disrupts both. It inhibits the thinking brain, and it makes us fear and doubt our intuitive reactions.

Noticing is a very different kind of brain function; it is the activity of being aware in this present moment. We cannot notice the past because it already happened, and we cannot notice the future because it is not here yet. All we can notice is our reaction to thinking about the past or the future in this present moment. But to notice with awareness requires the medial prefrontal cortex, the part of your brain described in the last chapter, located right behind the center of your forehead. Brain scan technology shows that the medial prefrontal cortex has connections to both the left and right sides of the brain, as well as to the lower levels associated with emotion, gut reaction, and impulse. Most importantly, researchers have shown that when individuals meditate, activity in the medial prefrontal cortex increases and, along with that, activity in the amygdala decreases. You may remember from earlier chapters that the amygdala functions to achieve two goals: to detect threat and to store emotional memories. The more stimulated the amygdala is, the more nervous and on guard we will feel. In addition, an activated amygdala increases sensitivity to triggers and stimulates impulsive urges. We are also more likely to experience increased flooding of trauma-related emotional and body memories. When flooding occurs, we might suddenly feel overwhelmed by anxiety, hopelessness, dread, or sadness without knowing why—a state that can last for hours and days at a time. When the amygdala is calmer, our nervous system is more regulated, and we can more easily tolerate stress and emotion. Flooding decreases when the amygdala is less stimulated and the window of tolerance expands.

The diagram in Figure 5.2 shows how different areas in the frontal cortex help us function throughout the day. Working memory is a function of the left brain, as are abilities such as long-term memory (memory for facts and other verbal information) and autobiographical memory (memory for what has happened in our lives). The working memory area of the left brain allows us to hold new information in mind and to connect it to other related ideas, words, or experiences. When we ask ourselves, "What should I do?" our working memory centers are stimulated to think of all the pros and cons, to consider information about similar decisions we have made before, and even to anticipate consequences based on what we have experienced in the past. Insight is another ability provided by the working memory areas of the brain, and so are activities like remembering a phone number or where we last put the car keys. These structures have no direct connection to the amygdala, so insight does not reduce activity in a traumatized amygdala. At times, insights may have a calming effect if they are compassionate or comforting, or if they reassure us that we are not crazy or defective, but they do not diminish traumatic responses.

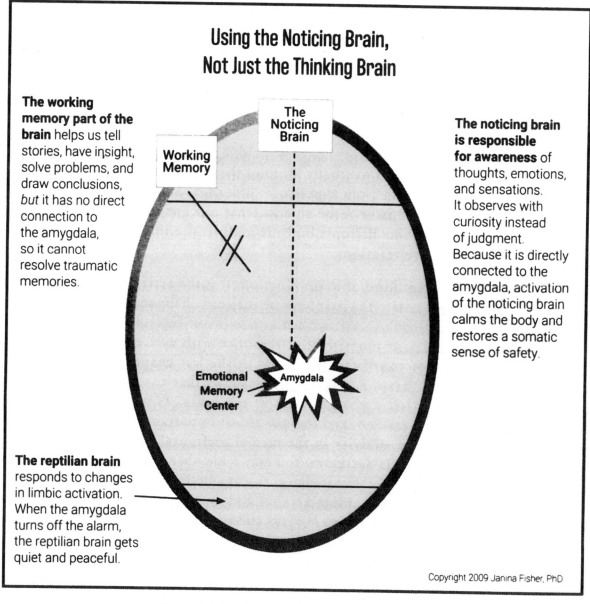

Figure 5.2: Getting Help from the Mindful Brain

> **Worksheet 13: How Working Memory Interprets Our Experience**
> will help you study the relationship between your negative thoughts
> and interpretations and your feelings and impulses. What types of
> interpretations and judgments do you usually make? And how does
> each affect your feeling and bodily state?

The noticing brain or medial prefrontal cortex, however, *does* connect directly to the amygdala, facilitating a calming effect when we are more mindful and when we notice rather than commenting on what we notice. For trauma survivors, free-floating meditation is not always the right approach to increasing activity in the medial prefrontal cortex. Internal awareness can sometimes be very triggering, so it is usually more helpful to start using the noticing brain to notice very specific things. For example, when a feeling of anxiety comes up, noticing it as just anxiety or as just a body sensation (increased heartbeat or tightening in the chest or stomach) or as "just triggering" usually helps to regulate the anxiety. When feelings of shame get triggered, remembering to notice the physical sensations of the shame and the thoughts that go with it as separate components is usually calming or regulating. In mindful noticing, we do not get flooded with the feeling—we notice it at a very slight distance, even as something interesting or curious.

It requires practice to notice a feeling instead of reacting to it by drawing conclusions or assigning blame. Most of us interpret our feelings as quickly as we have them. We might feel embarrassed and then interpret that as a sign of having done something stupid. We feel sadness, and then we interpret it as either weakness or a sign of how much we have lost or how terribly we have been treated. These interpretations very rarely make us feel better!

Noticing the shame, sadness, anxiety, or anger without judgment or interpretation has a very different effect. Noticing sadness means bringing our attention to the choked-up feeling in the throat, the wetness or tears in the eyes, and the emotional pain in the chest. When we notice the sensations of pain rather than recall all the experiences that have caused the pain, it has a slightly calming effect. If we notice the tears instead of interpreting them as weakness, they will subside much more easily than if we try to choke them back. Whenever we notice a feeling as just a feeling or a thought as just a thought, it is generally less overwhelming.

In the mindfulness world, meditators are taught to observe with interest and "without attachment or aversion." These words speak to the very human tendency we all have to agree with certain thoughts and feelings and to push other feelings away or reject them. We might agree with the thought "Your opinion doesn't matter" and reject the thought "Whatever I think or feel does matter," judging it as too grandiose or narcissistic. Mindful noticing disciplines us to be aware of each thought with equal curiosity: "I'm having the thought that I should shut up—my opinion doesn't matter anyway—and now I'm having another thought that everyone's opinion matters." With the noticing brain, we might then observe that the thought "My opinion doesn't matter" is followed by a slump in the shoulders and a sigh, then a feeling of heaviness and defeat. Or we might notice that thinking, "My feelings and opinions do matter" is accompanied by spontaneously sitting up straight and holding the head higher or by a feeling of confidence or solidness. The noticing brain does not judge either thought—it just notices that the negative thought feels more familiar and the positive thought more unfamiliar or even unpleasant. It can be used to notice which feels better or lightens our sense of carrying a load.

USING THE NOTICING BRAIN TO CHANGE HABITUAL PATTERNS

Because activating the medial prefrontal cortex reduces activity in the amygdala and therefore calms and regulates the nervous system, the noticing brain is a game-changer in the struggle with addictive or unsafe behavior. It allows us to study compulsive impulses without judgment or shame. Noticing what happens when we act on unsafe impulses is also crucial to interrupting the Abstinence/Relapse Cycle. Even better, noticing the negative consequences of a relapse without attachment or aversion also helps stabilize unsafe behavior and addictive patterns.

> Use **Worksheet 14: Getting Help from the Noticing Brain** to observe the differences between what happens when you notice and what happens when you analyze or judge your thoughts and feelings. Does noticing an impulse without judging it or trying to control it make it easier to avoid acting on it? Does noticing make intense emotions easier to tolerate?

The key is increasing your ability to notice your thoughts, feelings, and impulses as signals about how the nervous system is doing, rather than a sign of how you are measuring up to old expectations. Are you activated or shut down? Overwhelmed or numb? Or is your window of tolerance expansive enough to tolerate whatever you are feeling? What do the thoughts, feelings, and impulses tell you about where you are on the Abstinence/Relapse Cycle?

Keep in mind that the goal is to regulate your nervous system so that you can tolerate your moment-to-moment feelings and thoughts. All human beings will experience unpleasant, overwhelming emotions and impulses at points in their lives, and we all need to have the bandwidth to tolerate these ups and downs. Trauma makes that challenge much harder because the body responses and feeling memories are so easily triggered on a daily basis, disrupting the sense of present time. Although the eating disorder, self-harm, or suicidal thoughts and feelings may have been ways of managing triggered response, you are reading this chapter because they no longer work so well or are causing new difficulties and risks.

No treatment approach, skill, or intervention can make the feelings just go away, and even the eating disorder, addiction, or self-destructive actions eventually stop having that instantaneous effect. All we human beings are left with are "10% solutions": things that help us 5%, 10%, or 15% of the time or that help for a few minutes while we are doing them. Most ways of healthy coping are 10% solutions: taking a moment to breathe, focusing on something that feels better, reading a book or watching television, filling out a worksheet, going for a walk, knitting, crocheting, doing crossword puzzles, gardening, taking a hot bath, reciting the Serenity Prayer, or playing with a pet or with children. Even psychotherapy is a 10% solution, and so are most psychiatric medications and coping skills. Very few coping habits are immediately and completely effective. To feel better at bad times, we might have to use five or ten different solutions until we begin to feel a little relief.

> Use **Worksheet 15: 10% Solutions** to develop an ongoing list of what helps to give you 5% or 10% relief. You will begin to see patterns. For example, you might notice that you get a 10% solution from physical activities that involve working with your hands, activities that require concentration and focus without a lot of thinking (like jigsaw puzzles or knitting), or activities that involve contact with other human beings or with pets. You can cultivate more solutions in any category that seems to be a good fit for you as an individual, or you can integrate skills that you have learned to add to your list of solutions. And keep this worksheet handy during hard days so you can remind yourself of things you can do to get through the day—10% at a time.

In an ideal world, you would have grown up in a safe, supportive environment where your needs for reassurance and soothing were met by parents who felt your distress and were relieved when you felt better. Your nervous system would have learned how to recover from ups and downs, and your "emotional muscles" would have had a chance to grow stronger. But a traumatic environment, as we will see in the next chapter, robs children of what they need in order to develop a resilient nervous system and a wide, flexible window of tolerance, making the trauma-related feeling and body memories even harder to manage and tolerate. Sadly, one very unfair aspect of recovering from trauma is the fact that now, as an adult, you have to work so hard to develop the capacities that should have been facilitated or taught to you as a small child. As unjust as it is, however, it is more unfair to continue feeling numb, overwhelmed, or constantly frightened, angry, and ashamed. Working your emotional muscles by practicing 10% solutions will help to give you the window of tolerance you need for a life after trauma.

The next chapter will help you to understand more about traumatic attachment and its "living legacy."

Tracking Your Abstinence/Relapse Cycle

Write in what you notice at each stage of the cycle. How do you feel when you first get sober or abstain from unsafe actions? Then, what are the signs that your PTSD symptoms are worsening? What tells you that you are having unsafe impulses again? How do relapses usually happen? And then what? Do not judge yourself! Be curious and interested in the cycle that has driven you so many times.

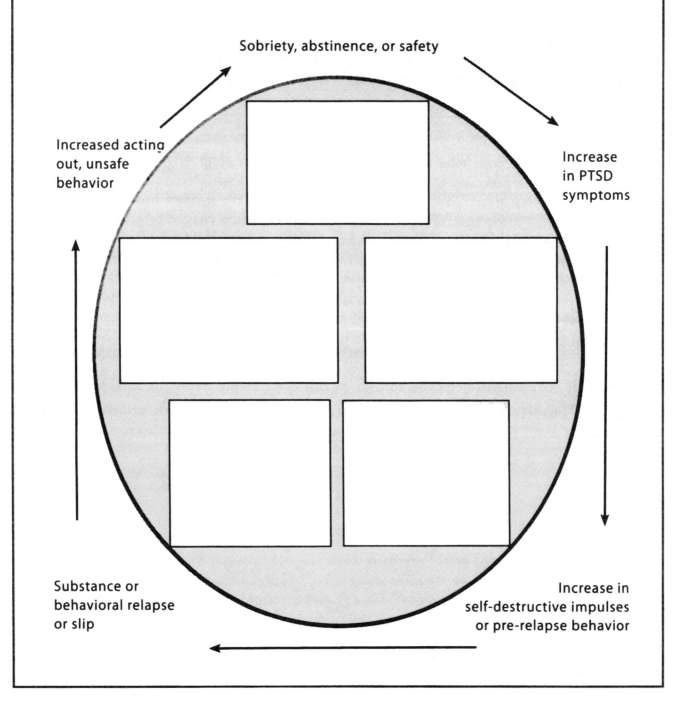

Sobriety, abstinence, or safety

Increased acting out, unsafe behavior

Increase in PTSD symptoms

Substance or behavioral relapse or slip

Increase in self-destructive impulses or pre-relapse behavior

Breaking the Cycle

Because the brain and body tend to default to old patterns under stress, you may notice the same cycle occurring each time you try to use new healthier coping strategies. Write in what you notice when you try to change trauma-related patterns.

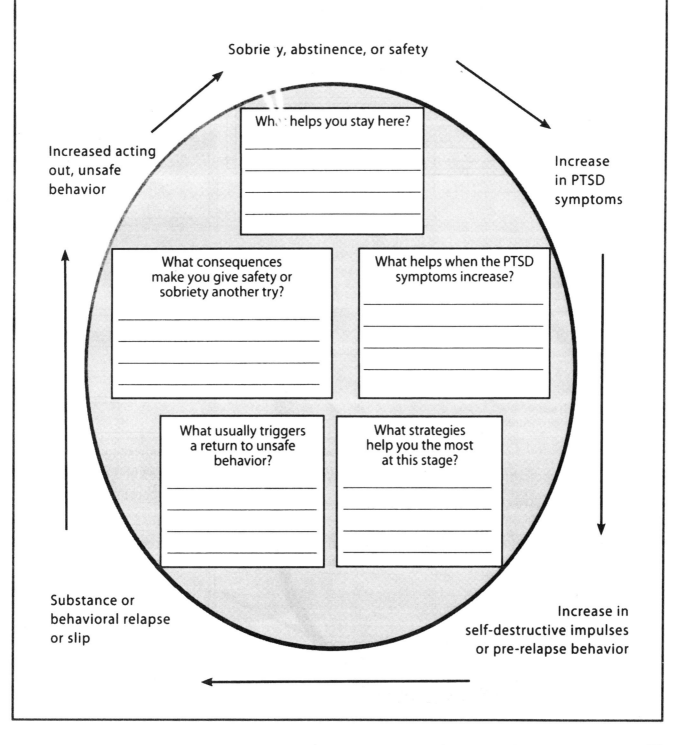

Sobriety, abstinence, or safety

Increased acting out, unsafe behavior

Increase in PTSD symptoms

What helps you stay here?

What consequences make you give safety or sobriety another try?

What helps when the PTSD symptoms increase?

What usually triggers a return to unsafe behavior?

What strategies help you the most at this stage?

Substance or behavioral relapse or slip

Increase in self-destructive impulses or pre-relapse behavior

How Working Memory Interprets Our Experience

Write in the kinds of interpretations that your working memory usually makes when you feel distress. Then notice. Do the feelings get better or worse? Do your sensations and impulses increase or decrease?

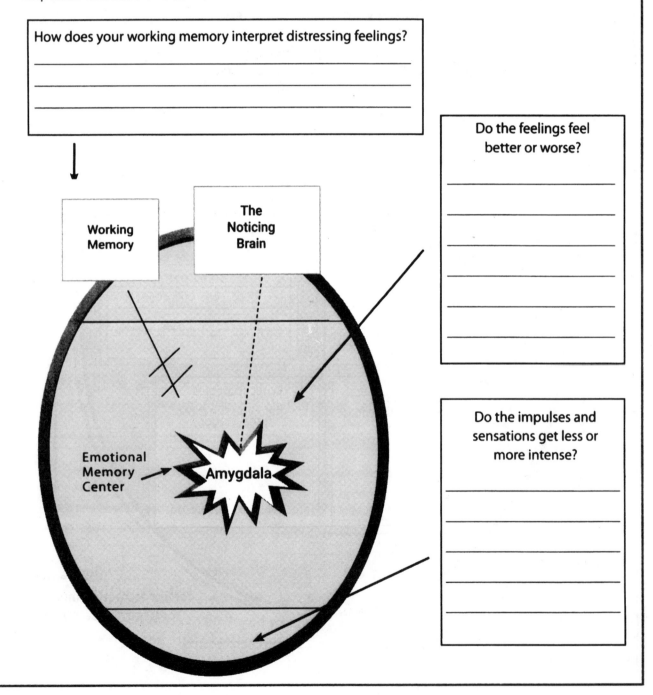

How does your working memory interpret distressing feelings?

_____
_____
_____

Working Memory

The Noticing Brain

Emotional Memory Center

Amygdala

Do the feelings feel better or worse?

_____
_____
_____
_____
_____
_____

Do the impulses and sensations get less or more intense?

_____
_____
_____
_____
_____

Getting Help from the Noticing Brain

What is different when you use your noticing brain? What happens when you use your noticing brain to observe your feelings, thoughts, and body sensations without judgment?

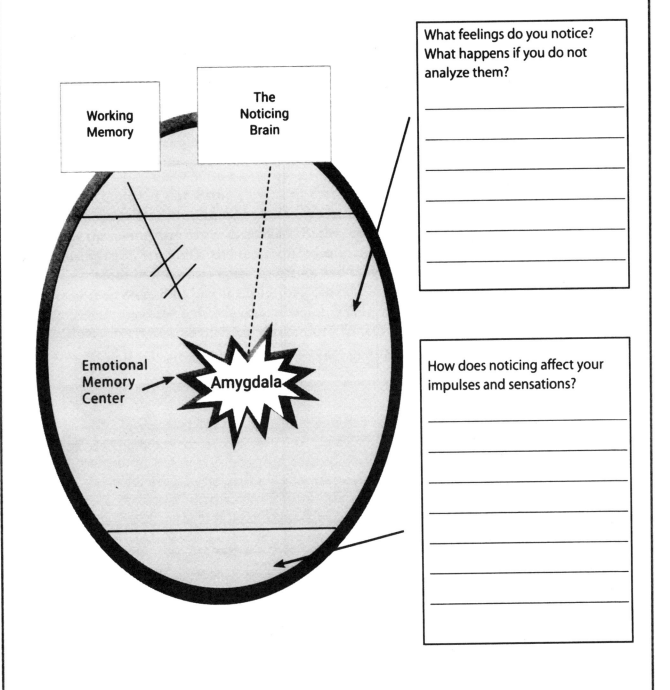

Working Memory

The Noticing Brain

Emotional Memory Center

Amygdala

What feelings do you notice? What happens if you do not analyze them?

_____
_____
_____
_____
_____
_____
_____

How does noticing affect your impulses and sensations?

_____
_____
_____
_____
_____
_____
_____

10% Solutions

Any activity that gives me even a little bit of relief or pleasure or takes my mind off negative thoughts	What % does it help?	What kinds of feelings, thoughts, situations, and impulses does it help with?

6

Trauma and Attachment

Unlike other animals, human babies begin life with a very immature brain and body, sometimes struggling to keep up a steady heartbeat and breathing. Because their nervous systems are so underdeveloped, they lack the capacity to eat, sleep, change positions, and regulate their emotional and physical states without round-the-clock help from their caretakers. Ideally, during this stage of development, loving, attuned parents do more than help children by feeding them and keeping them physically comfortable. They also help babies recover from distress, expand their capacity to sustain positive feelings, and teach them how to communicate their physical and interpersonal needs. Good attachment teaches us that it is safe to be soothed by others *and* that it is safe to soothe ourselves when loved ones are not available. Even the child's ability to acquire new information, problem solve, and verbally communicate is dependent upon the quality of parental attachment.

Early attachment is not a single event or even a series of particular events. It is the result of hundreds of physical and emotional experiences: being held, rocked, fed, stroked, or soothed, and experiencing the loving gaze of our caretakers. Rather than using words, loving parents communicate to infants using coos, mmmm's, and terms of endearment that evoke a lilt in the voice of the speaker. Young children take in the warm eyes, the smile, and the playfulness, and they respond with sounds and smiles of their own. But, just as easily, they can take in the caregiver's bodily tension, stony face, rough movements, and the irritable tone of voice. Their immature nervous systems are alarmed by bright lights, loud sounds, or physical discomfort, so it is not surprising that sudden movements, intense emotional reactions, loud voices, and anger or anxiety are all frightening for babies.

Use **Worksheet 16: Noticing Your Reactions to Closeness and Distance** at this point to notice your own reactions to closeness and distance. Write in the key things you learned about closeness and distance as a child, such as "It was not safe to be close," "Mother couldn't tolerate my distance," "I had to be seen and not heard," "We got punished," or "My parents couldn't tolerate closeness to anyone, even their children." Then write in the key things you notice in your relationships. Do you feel comfortable being close? To whom does it feel comfortable to be close? (Some individuals feel comfortable being close to their children but not to a spouse—or to friends or a spouse but not their siblings.) How do you do with distance? Is that easier or harder?

HOW WE REMEMBER ATTACHMENT

Whether our parents promote a sense of safety or they frighten us, no child remembers these experiences of attachment in words or as individual events. In the first three years of life, attachment is primarily remembered in the form of nonverbal body memories: emotional, physical, autonomic, tactile, visual, or auditory memories—memories without words. Our attachment or relationship styles are also memories of how we adapted to the relational environment of our childhoods. If we were held lovingly and safely, we feel comfortable hugging others or being hugged by them. If we were held in a frightening or abusive way, our bodies might tighten up when people come close to us or tense and pull away even when we are touched in a perfectly safe way. Closeness or physical contact may trigger a surge of fear. Whether we like to snuggle or prefer less physical contact, whether we smile or have no expression, look away rather than at people, like we-time more than me-time or vice versa, our relational habits were formed very early in life.

EYE-TO-EYE COMMUNICATION

Babies are born with the instinct to seek the eyes of the person caring for them. Their heads turn until they see the attachment figure looking at them, and then their eyes lock on to that gaze. Research shows that infants even prefer to look at pictures of eyes when there are no human faces or eyes at which to gaze.

But what if the eyes of the baby's caregivers are scary eyes? What if they frighten the child? The majority of adults gaze at babies with warm, loving, interested eyes—but what if the parent is high or sedated on drugs? What if the attachment figure has a mental illness and is preoccupied with voices, images, or fears in his or her head? What if the parent's eyes reflect rage at having to take care of a baby twenty-four hours a day? Despite their innate preference for gazing, most babies have the same instinctive response to things that startle or disturb them: They close their eyes and turn their heads away. Years later, looking into the eyes of a partner, a loved one, or even a therapist may still evoke fear and gaze aversion.

This is well illustrated through Cathy's experience:

> Cathy said to me one day, "I notice that I can't look at you—it's weird. You're looking at me, and I'm looking off to the side of you. It's not that I don't like you or trust you because I do, but it's just hard to look into your eyes."

Kaitlin's example also illustrates how can attachment trauma can elicit gaze aversion:

> Kaitlin consistently turned her head to look out the office window while we were talking. Curious about this pattern, I voiced it one day, "I notice your eyes are focused on the window—even when we're talking—and I'm curious about that." She looked at me as if I were stupid, "Of course—because that's the window I'm going to jump out of when they come for me."

Their habits of eye contact were trauma-related, not personal to me or anyone else in their lives. Kaitlin was always looking for an escape route, and Cathy had grown up looking into the eyes of the depressed mother she loved so much and seeing a far-away, hopeless expression. Years later, their brains and their bodies were still remembering what was safe then and what was not.

TOLERATING CLOSENESS AND DISTANCE

If we feel safety in closeness to our attachment figures when we are very young and then we later learn to feel safe when they are in another room or at work or preoccupied, the capacity to tolerate being close to others expands and so does the ability to tolerate being separated or out of contact. We grow up to become adults who might prefer more contact or more distance, but we can tolerate less of either when necessary.

In a traumatic environment, there is no safe place. Closeness is rarely safe, but neither is being alone because a child is unprotected when no safe adult is present. Showing emotion is rarely safe either because a child's sadness or anger usually triggers abusive and neglectful parents to lash out. Needs are not safe because normal needs for care and closeness can be exploited. It is not safe to trust reassurance, and it is certainly not safe to allow abusive parents to comfort us. It is not safe when abusive parents show affection either—nor is it safe to demonstrate loving feelings toward them. Every single aspect of close relationships can become dangerous in a traumatic environment. Figure 6.1 depicts the way in which safe attachment builds the capacity for both closeness and autonomy while unsafe attachments create a sense that either is dangerous.

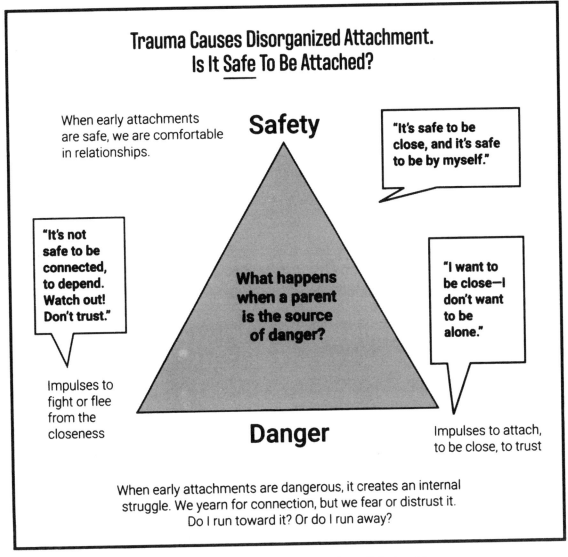

Figure 6.1: What Trauma Teaches Us about Relationships

If the abuser is a parent, then the home is not safe, and the only safe place is at school or at a grandparent's house. In that situation, children learn to fear or avoid family relationships and feel safe only at a distance from others. Equally frightening is the experience of the home and attachment figures offering a safe place while the child encounters danger outside of the family (e.g., when abused or exploited by neighbors, babysitters, teachers, coaches, or extended family members). That teaches children that it is safe to be close but not safe to be away from home or in the company of other people. Because we were too young to remember why and how we developed the habits and reactions we have, it can be very confusing when these traumatic attachment patterns follow us into adulthood.

FRIGHTENED AND FRIGHTENING PARENTING

Research shows that children can be traumatized even when there is no abuse in the family. Having parents who are frightening or appear frightened (who are anxious, withdrawn, phobic, depressed, or shut down) creates a sense of danger for the young child. It is scary to have a frightened parent and, of course, scary to have a frightening parent. But for children, it can be even more confusing and distressing because a child's natural biological response to feeling scared is to seek the attachment figure, to move closer. The problem is that moving closer to a frightening or frightened parent is scary too, and the body's other natural response is to move away from something frightening.

When the person to whom the traumatized child is drawn to find safety is also the danger from which he or she is seeking refuge, the child is literally caught between a rock and a hard place. The instinct to cling to the attachment figure when alarmed also triggers the child's instinct to pull back, but then the pulling back triggers the instinct to move closer, which then increases the instinct to pull back. Sometimes children have a "fight" response to a neglectful, abusive parent and feel the impulse to push away angrily. Whenever either parent is frightened or frightening, the instinct to cling or move closer is activated, and as the child gets close enough to get hurt, the fight-or-flight instinct is evoked.

Because the children of frightening and frightened parents are chronically afraid of being hurt, they are sensitive to many things that can be better tolerated by children who feel safe. Any small or large rejection, being misunderstood, being told no, being disappointed, failures of empathy, or being "on the outside looking in" can trigger intense emotional and physical alarm reactions: fear, shame, emotional pain, anger. The closer the relationship, the more intense these triggered responses, a phenomenon that is often misunderstood by teachers, adoptive parents, and other adults in the child's life. The teacher or adoptive parent might hope that with increasing closeness will come increasing trust, only to find that the opposite occurs. Many survivors with these traumatic attachment patterns have very good, stable friendships but get triggered in their intimate partner relationships. Others also get triggered in friendships or in family relationships with non-offending parents and siblings.

Trauma survivors frequently find themselves fleeing from those who are kindest to them and attaching to partners who are distant or even abusive. They blame themselves for these patterns ("Why do I always choose abusive men?") without understanding their origin in early traumatic attachment. But the dynamics make perfect sense in a trauma context: A distant or abusive partner triggers the instinct to seek closeness, while the caring, safe partner, who wants to be close, automatically triggers the impulse to flee or fight.

If this is a pattern that is familiar to you, it is important to reassure yourself that these are very natural trauma-related reactions, not a sign that you make bad choices. The most important thing you can do to transform these patterns is to observe them. Be curious: Notice when you feel strong needs for closeness or when closeness is triggering for you, observe impulses to distance or push others away, and become aware of what gets triggered in you when others respond by distancing or defending themselves or getting angry.

Annie's parents were frightening, and they were abusive: Her father was superficially charming but sexually abusive, and her mother was physically and emotionally abusive. In addition, her alcoholic mother often appeared frightened: passed out on the couch and unresponsive or nervous and irritable, or at other times in a violent rage. Annie had to adapt to this complex and very unsafe environment, care for her younger siblings, and keep them out of danger as much as she could. Her "go-to" pattern was caretaking: soothing her irritable mother and caring for her when she passed out, charming her teachers at school because they were the only adults who seemed to like her, and working hard to earn acceptance from her peers. But, internally, she instinctively pulled back and disconnected when around other people. She learned to hide from her parents—in the closet, outside in nature, or in the world of books.

As an adult, she could not make sense of her tendency to caretake everyone around her other than to assume that she was being pressured by others to meet their needs. She explained her tendency to isolate (especially when other people approached her for friendship) as a way of avoiding exploitation, and she assumed that her husband of thirty years did not really love her because he was not very emotionally expressive. She believed that, in fact, no one cared about her and, as a result, she could not recognize all the ways her husband, sons, and extended family demonstrated how much they loved her. She could not believe that she was the glue that held her family of choice together and attributed their seeking her out as a bid for caretaking. Stuck in the relational patterns dictated by her childhood situation, she felt alone, hurt, unloved, and unlovable.

Remember: A pattern always reflects memory. We learned that pattern somewhere, and if it is very familiar, we learned it when we were young. Do not put pressure on yourself to figure out where the pattern came from. Just assume that it was a necessary adaptation to the limitations of your attachment figures or that it was a survival strategy, just as it was for Annie.

> Use **Worksheet 17: Traumatic Attachment Patterns** to observe your patterns in relationships. Try not to be distracted by thoughts and feelings about the people to whom you have these reactions. It is more important to be curious about how the trauma has affected your capacity to be in relationships and to become aware of these patterns. Do your fight-or-flight responses get triggered by nice people or abusive people? Do you flee when people do not treat you well, or do you put up with it? Do you feel compelled to stay close to them because you are afraid to be alone?

CHANGING TRAUMATIC PATTERNS IN RELATIONSHIPS

Having seen some of your own patterns on Worksheet 17, you now have a chance to decide what changes you want to make. For example, you might see that the biggest problem you encounter in relationships is not being able to set boundaries, not being able to say no, tolerating abusive or inconsiderate behavior, and fearing abandonment or being left alone. Or you might notice a pattern of having walls up, feeling suffocated by too much closeness or niceness, not letting your partner in, and not sharing your thoughts and feelings other than in anger. Or you might see a pattern of seeking closeness when the other person is distant and seeking distance when they want to be close. You might notice that you have very high standards or needs in relationships and very little tolerance when your partner does not meet them. Are you quick to anger? Or quick to hurt? Or quick to hurt followed by anger?

> **Worksheet 18: Changing Our Attachment Patterns** will give you a chance to look at some of your patterns in close relationships, whether with friends, family, or romantic partners. Some of these patterns might be okay with you, and some may not. Do not judge them. Just note which ones are most problematic in your life. If there are many, then prioritize just two or three related ones. Next, assume that these patterns are triggered reactions. You might even want to start a Trigger Log so you can see the triggers in advance. Assume that you do not have a window of tolerance in relationships even if you have developed a window in other areas of your life. It is understandable: Relationships can feel like a safe haven or like the most dangerous undertaking of our lives.

Go back to some of your earlier worksheets. Do you need to expand your window of tolerance for closeness? Or for not being understood? Or for being disappointed or hurt? Or do you need to increase your ability to tolerate setting boundaries with your partner? Or work at tolerating your partner's quirks and bad habits? Remember that the abuse was not just ethically and morally wrong. It was also the abuser's bad habit, and therefore even harmless bad habits could be a very big trigger for you.

Yvonne was ready to give up family dinnertimes because she was so irritated by her husband's behavior. "My husband is so immature and irresponsible—how could he behave the way he does? How could he teach my son such terrible habits?"

I asked, "What exactly happens at the dinner table that makes you so angry?"

"They play with their food! They have little food fights! My husband puts some of his mashed potatoes on my son's plate, then my son puts his broccoli on my husband's plate, and then my husband puts more mashed potato on, and they think it's so funny, but it isn't!"

"And what would have happened to you," I said, "if you and your siblings had done that at the dinner table?"

"We would have been beaten within an inch of our lives—that would have been stupid and dangerous!"

Then I understood. "No wonder you're triggered by their food fights! It feels like they are doing something really unsafe, and they're not aware of it, and they are not stopping." Yvonne was alarmed by what would have been dangerous to her years ago, rather than amused to see her husband and son bonding in such an annoying but harmless way.

What helped Yvonne to change her pattern was to keep reminding herself that she was just triggered. Nothing bad was happening—no one was getting hurt or punished. When she just kept saying to herself, "I'm triggered—that's all that's happening," over and over again, she could feel her heart rate going down and the anger subsiding.

As she anticipated another stressful dinner time, she realized that she could simply explain to them that the food fighting was making her nervous. She did not have to criticize them and make them both feel defensive. Her husband's pattern was to be passive and conflict avoidant in relationships, so he rarely protested her criticisms, but he would withdraw and become very quiet. That felt safer to her, but she knew that the result was more distance between them. They were both keeping things safe the way they knew safety as children, but that was not keeping them close.

Without seeing the patterns, most people keep blaming themselves or their partners. Yvonne could have blamed the failure of closeness on her husband, but seeing the whole pattern helped her to see that he was triggered by her alarm and her judgments of him, just as she was triggered by both his playfulness and his withdrawal. She still felt some alarm when he and her son got silly at the dinner table as her body remembered how violent her stepfather used to get when he was irritated by her brothers, but she no longer interpreted the alarm as a clear and present danger.

Remember: It takes practice to change our habits of surviving! Insight is not enough to create lasting change.

Practice noticing and naming when something is triggering for you—over and over and over again: "I'm triggered—this is very triggering—I'm really triggered." Consider the possibility that what you find offensive (unless illegal or immoral) is related to triggers more than to the actual degree of badness inherent in the action. For example, many individuals find themselves wanting to flee relationships or even threatening to leave their mates when they are triggered. Is that "mean"? Or is it an automatic reaction triggered by the relational dynamics? Many individuals get quiet when they are hurt or angry—or get loud and accusatory—or walk away. Or they try to "improve" their partners by critiquing behavior that triggers them. These patterns reflect what our bodies and emotions learned about relationships long ago. They do not usually reflect conscious, thoughtful choices.

Assume that unless your partner has beaten you, publicly humiliated you, kept you confined to your home, controlled your ability to come and go, or harmed you or your children, you are probably triggered by his or her behavior. Be curious. How am I triggering my partner? Are we both triggering each other? Awareness of triggering is another important ingredient in healthy relationships. We cannot always prevent our partners and spouses from getting triggered, but we can make an effort to avoid triggering them when there is a choice to say or do something a little differently. Learning how to be sensitive to the other person's triggers without feeling like you are walking on eggshells or automatically complying is very healthy in relationships. We tend to do that naturally with children, friends, or someone more vulnerable than ourselves, but we often forget to do that with our partners.

HOW MUCH SHOULD I TOLERATE?

It is hard for all human beings to know the limits of what they should accept or tolerate. There is no absolute standard other than a legal one. We have a legal right not to accept physically or sexually violent treatment, the use of weapons to enforce control, physical restraint, threatening behavior, drug use, or other self-destructive actions that threaten our safety or that of our children. Beyond that, it becomes hard, especially for trauma survivors, to discern what is unacceptable or unsafe and what is just insensitive and rude behavior. (If you question whether or not you are being abused, there are many checklists available online that can guide you in assessing what feels like abuse in your relationship.) Often, financial dependence on one's partner can bias us into accepting inappropriate behavior as something we have to tolerate. Or if we are triggered by rude, uncaring, or insensitive behavior, we may not be able to access a sense of deserving or having a right to set boundaries or even walk away.

One standard to determine how much to put up with is to ask, "Are the negatives I get worth whatever positives I get?" If you are with someone flawed but non-abusive whom you deeply love, it might be worth learning to manage all the triggering in the relationship. If you are in the job of your dreams, it might be worth the effort to work with all the triggering that comes with it. All human beings have the right to determine how much they choose to tolerate and when—they do not have to justify their choices.

> Jennifer was married to a man who adored her and supported her as a mother and professional, but he was also controlling and critical. In his prestigious job, he was respected as an expert and obeyed as a leader. Unfortunately, he brought those expectations home with him. He was always sure he was right and, if irritated or anxious, he would talk over her. He could not take Jennifer's opinions or feelings seriously unless they agreed with his. When friends asked her, "How can you put up with him?" she would always smile and say, "He adores me—he would do anything for me. I know he's just being a grumpy grump—it doesn't hurt me."

Jennifer made a choice that was not dictated by fear or shame. She did not feel smaller because, even though her husband sometimes belittled her, she did not *feel* belittled. That is the key.

Trauma survivors need to feel safe in order to heal; they need to feel some sense of control over their lives now; and they do not need to feel small or less than others or ashamed. At the same time, feeling memories of being small and ashamed, unloved and unwanted, or afraid and unsafe are inevitably going to be triggered even in good relationships, as Annie's example illustrates:

> Annie described her husband as uncaring and exploitive: "Why do I always have to make dinner? Why doesn't he ever make dinner for me? Why am I the one

who always has to bring up issues? Why am I the only one who cares about this relationship?" She could not take in that he showed his caring in other ways: by supporting the family through all the years that she was disabled by her PTSD symptoms, by never criticizing or questioning her triggered reactions, by helping her to do things that she was afraid to do alone, and by never touching her in any way without her permission first. He accepted her working when she could, not working when she could not, never tried to control her, and almost never got angry even when she would threaten to leave him. Not a very demonstrative man, he did not know how to express his feelings, and that failure of expression triggered Annie's feeling memories of a childhood in which no adult showed any genuine interest in or affection for her. His failure to cook for her or take care of her in more nurturing ways evoked feeling memories of the neglect she had also suffered. Her mother fed the children only when she was in the mood to do so, and often they went hungry. "I feel ashamed when I always have to cook for myself," she said. "It's like I'm not good enough—there's no one who cares if I eat or not."

It was liberating and comforting for Annie when she was able to see that she had been so triggered that she could not see the healthiness and caring in her marriage for many years. "I still wish he was a more emotional person," she would say, "but I know now it's not about me. He's just limited." Appreciating her marriage also helped her appreciate herself. "I was a mess when I met him, and I could have picked a monster, but I didn't."

TAKING CARE OF THE LITTLE "YOU" INSIDE

Being neglected and abused in childhood means that no one took care of that tiny child we all once were. In relationships, those young parts of all of us will get activated. We will feel uncomfortably vulnerable at times, and because our partners also feel vulnerable, they cannot always help us with the feelings they evoke in us. When Annie was triggered and felt the shame of the young Annie whose mother did not bother to feed her unless she was in the mood to do so, she instinctively looked to her husband to comfort and ease those feelings. When Yvonne was triggered by playfulness at the dinner table, the little Yvonne felt alarm and looked to her husband to keep things safe. We all instinctively turn to our partners for the things we did not get as children without recognition that we are reacting to the past. Although it was important for Yvonne to tell her husband that it made her nervous when he and their son were "horsing around" at the dinner table, and important for Annie to communicate that she was not criticizing her husband but just letting him know she was triggered, it was also important that they accept and welcome their own young traumatized selves.

Even though both husbands were sensitive to what their partners had gone through as children, the child parts could not take in that information. Years of abuse, neglect, rejection, and abandonment had left their mark. Even though each woman had married a very safe, accepting man, each still experienced the feeling memories on a daily basis. Each needed to welcome and make room for that wounded child inside, rather than trying to make the feeling memories go away by recruiting their husbands as caretakers.

In the next chapter, we will talk about how traumatic experiences leave individuals fragmented and their wounded child selves disowned and unwelcome.

Noticing Your Reactions
to Closeness and Distance

What did you learn about
closeness as a child?

_____

_____

_____

_____

_____

What happens when
you get close now?

_____

_____

_____

_____

_____

_____

_____

Safety

**Parent
Figure**

Danger

What did you learn about
keeping a distance from others?

_____

_____

_____

_____

_____

_____

What happens when
there is more distance now?

_____

_____

_____

_____

_____

_____

Traumatic Attachment Patterns

Recognizing the signs of traumatic attachment can help us in adult relationships. Am I putting up with too much? Or am I not willing to put up with anything? Am I confusing my partner with my reactions to distance and closeness? Do I need to leave this relationship, or am I just triggered?

Check the signs of traumatic attachment that you recognize:

☐ Difficulty with not being listened to

☐ Difficulty when people don't understand me

☐ Worrying that he or she doesn't love me

☐ Fear of being abandoned

☐ Fear of being cheated on

☐ Not wanting to be touched

☐ Wanting to be held all the time; only feeling safe when someone is there

☐ Worrying I'm not good enough

☐ Worrying the other person isn't good enough for me

☐ Wanting to leave bad relationships but I can't

☐ Wanting to run away when we get close

☐ Can't bear being alone/apart

☐ Feeling suffocated

☐ Putting up with abusive behavior

☐ Unable to put up with rude behavior

☐ Not letting my partner in; unable to share feelings

☐ Feeling rage when feelings are hurt

☐ Feeling unlovable

☐ Unable to tolerate partner's anger

☐ Unable to tolerate partner's silence

☐ Unable to set boundaries or say, "This is not okay"

Remember that these patterns developed as a way to survive when you were very young. They were the best you could do in a bad situation.

Changing Our Attachment Patterns

Not every survival pattern *has* to be changed. Check those that, if changed, would help you to have easier or better relationships.

Preference for Distance:

- [ ] Wanting to run away when we get close
- [ ] Feeling suffocated
- [ ] Not trusting my partner
- [ ] Believing I'm being cheated on
- [ ] Not wanting to be touched
- [ ] Feeling rage when feelings are hurt
- [ ] Worrying the other person is not good enough for me
- [ ] Unable to tolerate neediness, sadness, or insecurity in my partner
- [ ] Not putting up with rude or insensitive behavior
- [ ] Getting angry, pushing my partner away
- [ ] Stop talking when I'm upset

Preference for Closeness:

- [ ] Unable to bear being alone/apart
- [ ] Difficulty with not being listened to
- [ ] Putting up with abusive behavior
- [ ] Difficulty when people don't understand me or aren't concerned
- [ ] Worrying that he or she doesn't love me or that I'm going to be betrayed
- [ ] Fear of being abandoned
- [ ] Wanting to be held all the time; only feeling safe when someone is there
- [ ] Feeling unlovable when my feelings are hurt
- [ ] Unable to tolerate anger or silence
- [ ] Unable to set boundaries or say, "This is not okay"

Assume that these are triggered reactions. What happens when you notice them as just signs that you are triggered? What changes?

7

Trauma-Related Fragmentation and Dissociation

Without caretakers who are capable of creating safety, soothing distress, and caring for their physical well-being, small children must depend on their brains and bodies to manage the overwhelming reactions provoked by a threatening world. Many individuals recall, "There was never a day that I wasn't afraid or ashamed" or "My most vivid memory of childhood is the feeling of hunger—I was always hungry" or "I was always alone—always lonely and scared."

How does a very young child cope?

Luckily, the human brain and body have resources upon which even a baby can draw. We can dissociate, go numb and limp, or disconnect from our bodies. And our minds can split or fragment. With brains that are compartmentalized already, fragmenting is not difficult (Fisher, 2017).

HOW THE STRUCTURE OF THE BRAIN FACILITATES FRAGMENTATION

The brain as a whole is divided structurally into two major regions: the right hemisphere and the left hemisphere, each with very different functions and abilities. Though babies are born with both sides of the brain intact, they are right-brain dominant for most of childhood and rely on subcortical structures that drive action and emotion. The slower developing left brain has spurts of growth around age two and again at adolescence, but the development of left-brain dominance is only achieved very gradually over the course of childhood. For the two sides of the brain to talk to each other, a third area is required called the corpus callosum, a long narrow structure located between them. In childhood, right-brain experience is relatively independent of left-brain experience and vice versa, making fragmentation easy should the need for it arise. From research comparing the brains of traumatized children and teens with those of non-traumatized young people, we know that trauma seems to be associated with a smaller-than-average corpus callosum—meaning that it is underdeveloped, interfering with the ability of the left and right brains to communicate or collaborate with each other. The result is that trauma survivors often find themselves with a left hemisphere that does not coordinate well with the right hemisphere and vice versa.

As Figure 7.1 illustrates, the early developing right hemisphere is a nonverbal area of the brain, while the slower-to-develop left hemisphere has the ability for language and the capacity to remember experience chronologically and in words. The right brain is better at reading body language and facial expression, whereas the left brain is better at interpreting verbal language. The right brain remembers how things felt; the left brain remembers what happened. When we are triggered, the right hemisphere is more active; when we are planning and problem solving, the left hemisphere is more active. The result is a bit like having two different personalities: one logical, rational, and verbal but not in touch with emotion, and the other very emotional and reactive but not accessible to reason because it does not have words. All of

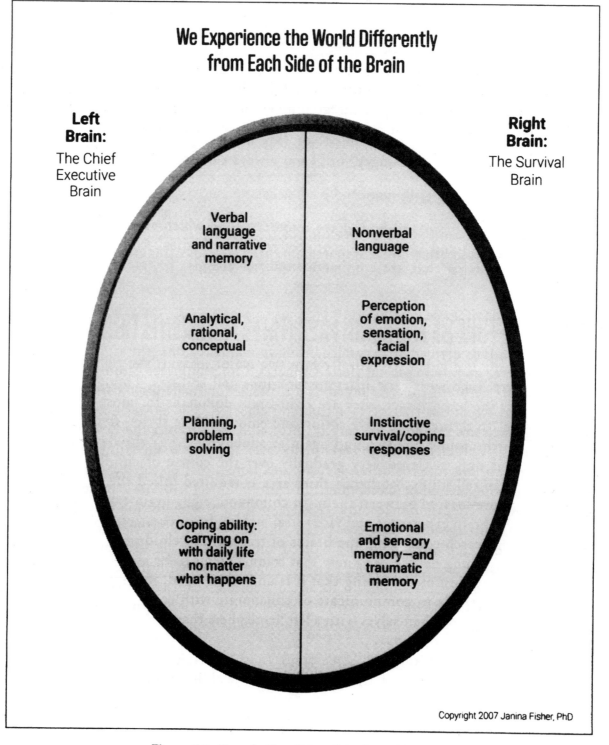

Figure 7.1: How the Two Sides of the Brain Function

us have had the experience of these two sides: We might be about to make an impulsive decision when the left brain stops us with its rationality. It reminds us that we might get caught or get hurt or that we might want to be a better person. Or we may be ill, grieving a loss, or undergoing a stressful time in our lives, and we question whether we can get through the day without breaking down, but somehow our ability to keep going instinctively kicks in, and we find ourselves able to think and function despite our distress.

UNDERSTANDING DISSOCIATED PARTS OF THE PERSONALITY

This biological situation is the foundation for a theory known as the Structural Dissociation Model developed by Onno van der Hart, Ellert Nijenhuis, and Kathy Steele (2006). It is a trauma model designed to make sense of individuals who have been chronically traumatized (e.g., have suffered multiple types of abuse and neglect at the hands of more than one perpetrator) or who have experienced familial abuse followed by other traumatic events.

The model theorizes that, in a traumatic environment, the more instinctive right brain is stimulated to anticipate danger by maintaining hypervigilance or readiness for action, while the left brain side of the personality "keeps on keeping on," getting through the day, keeping life going no matter what. This allows an abused child to be on guard and ready to hide but still able to walk to school, play with other children, and do homework. While the right-brain side might be afraid and ashamed, the left-brain side could be confidently developing skills as a student, athlete, artist, or scientist.

The diagram in Figure 7.2 represents this model of survival-related splitting. Under stress, the left- and right-brain sides of the personality begin to operate more independently to allow the individual to do two things at once: to carry on as if nothing has happened *and* to prepare for the next threat—and the next and the next. Both are necessary for survival. The authors of the Structural Dissociation theory named the left-brain self the "Apparently Normal Part of the Personality," suggesting that it pretends to be normal, but I quickly found that my clients could not appreciate the important role of this part of the personality when it was called "apparently normal." So, for their sakes, I re-named it the "Going On with Normal Life" self to emphasize that our left-brain selves reflect an instinctive survival-related drive to "keep on keeping on," not a false or pretend self. I wanted to emphasize the positive evolutionary function of this part and challenge the tendency to see the ability to function as a false self, as if the trauma-related responses were the only "true self."

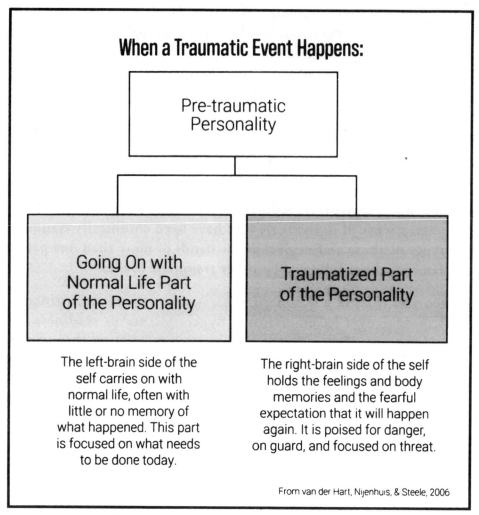

Figure 7.2: The Structural Dissociation Model

In addition, emphasizing the positive aims and goals of the Going On with Normal Life self encourages survivors to strengthen their ability to manage the tumultuous emotions of the defense-related parts, rather than simply trying to ignore them. We could think of the right-brain part of the personality as the Emotional Part, as do the authors of the theory, or we could think of it as the traumatized part of the personality. It can be very confusing and crazy-making to be logical, rational, and functional one minute and then be overwhelmed by emotion and impulse five minutes later. This model helps to reassure survivors that they are not crazy or faking it. They can learn to identify triggered reactions and overwhelming emotions as the traumatized part(s) and understand their Going On with Normal Life part as a resource, not a pseudo-self.

> *Tammy always struggled during her birthday month of July, alternately yearning for someone to care about her and then developing elaborate plans to commit suicide on the day itself. Some years, she was hospitalized because of her suicide risk or would miss many days of work because she could not get out of bed in the morning. One year, she was shocked to find out at the end of the month that she had won the Employee of the Month Award! Even though she had called in sick many times, she apparently had been extremely productive when she was there, more so than other workers who never missed a day of work. That was the first sign she ever had to indicate that she was more than her loneliness and suicidality.*

Use **Worksheet 19: The Structural Dissociation Model** to explore the two sides of you. Avoid labeling characteristics of either side as bad, shameful, or false. Just be curious about your inner struggles and which sides of your brain are in conflict.

MORE DANGER MEANS GREATER NEED FOR SPECIALIZED SURVIVAL-RELATED PARTS

The Structural Dissociation Model goes on to say that with repeated and chronic experiences of trauma, more complex splitting and fragmentation is often adaptive and necessary. But it too follows the logic of the body and brain. Because children have to depend upon their instinctive animal defense survival responses (fight and flight, cry for help, freeze in fear, or collapse and submit) in the absence of parental protection, the theory states that with chronic trauma, subparts of the personality spontaneously develop representing these very different forms of self-protection (see Figure 7.3). The model is clear that fragmentation or structural dissociation is a normal instinctive reaction to repeated trauma, not necessarily evidence of a dissociative disorder. You will be able to sense if these ideas resonate for you.

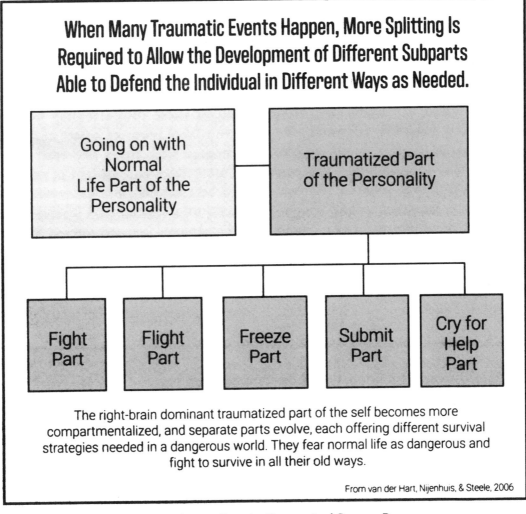

Figure 7.3: Understanding the Traumatized Parts as Protectors

For example, in some families, it is not safe for children to fight back or show anger, but having a fragmented, split-off fight part means that the anger does not have to be felt by the child and therefore is not perceived by the adults. In other families, it is even more dangerous for the child to cry or to cry for help (e.g., to tell other adults what is happening). Having a fragmented cry for help part allows the child to cry or show distress in some situations (e.g., with a grandparent or teacher) while never looking sad in the presence of the abusive parent. The cry for help part also seeks closeness and protection—both of which are dangerous with abusive parents. Fragmenting in this way allows for very complex and sophisticated adaptations to traumatic environments. The submit part might carry the sense of hopelessness and helplessness necessary in an environment where being seen and not heard is most adaptive and hope is risky, while the Going On with Normal Life part goes to school, plans ahead for college and then a life beyond trauma. And, as the Going On with Normal Life self is planning a future, the suicidal fight part might be plotting a way out if things get worse, and the flight part might be drinking too much to manage the hopelessness of the submit part and the flashbacks of the freeze or fear part.

> Carly had hopes and dreams for her future beginning when she was quite young. Then she met her partner in college at age 19 and began to imagine someday having a home and family and a career as a therapist. But these hopes and dreams were complicated by the daily nightmares and flashbacks she still experienced. These symptoms overwhelmed her and triggered a hopeless part that just wanted to give up. Unfortunately, that was usually a signal to her suicidal part to begin a new round of planning how to die rather than live with being constantly overwhelmed. "I don't think I want to die," she said. "I have a lot to live for. I don't understand why I keep trying to kill myself."

For children raised in unsafe environments, all of these subparts may be necessary in response to changing demands. For example, going to school requires a part of the personality that can pay attention in class, learn, and socially engage with peers and teachers. At home, with parents who may be withdrawn and neglectful sometimes and violent at others, different parts dedicated to different ways of surviving could be essential. For example, the sound of the abuser's voice or footsteps might trigger the panic of a fearful part (freeze), alerting the body to danger; a playful part might try to lift the parent's irritable mood and facilitate a positive connection by making him laugh (social engagement); a caretaker part (submission) might try to protect herself or her younger siblings in the face of the violent behavior; and a hypervigilant fight part would be carefully observing the parents' mood to anticipate how to best defend against them.

Use **Worksheet 20: Identifying the Traumatized Parts** to connect the parts model to your own particular symptoms and struggles. You do not have to be certain—just begin to be curious about which part of you is shy, which part is ashamed, which part is mistrustful, etc. See if this model intuitively makes sense to you, even if it is a very new idea.

Usually, the Going On with Normal Life part of any individual tries to carry on with daily priorities (e.g., functioning at a job, raising the children, caring for pets, organizing home life, even taking on meaningful personal and professional goals). But those activities are often complicated when traumatized parts are triggered in the context of everyday life, resulting in overwhelming emotions, incapacitating depression or anxiety, hypervigilance and mistrust, self-destructive behavior, and fear or hopelessness about the future. Many survivors come for treatment after being flooded or highjacked by the feelings and physiological reactions of the trauma-related parts; others come when their attempts to disconnect from or deny these responses lead to chronic depression or depersonalization.

Geraldine considered herself a successful survivor of her childhood. By the age of 38, she had left home, married her childhood sweetheart, established herself professionally, had a baby, and bought the house of her dreams. She felt that she had made it. She finally had everything she had ever wanted, and now she could finally relax. And then she woke up one day trembling with inexplicable and overwhelming fear, hopelessness, dread, and a feeling of desperation. The tsunami of trauma had hit, and the parts had highjacked her body. Not knowing what these feelings meant, she went to see a therapist who encouraged her to talk about her painful childhood past—which left her feeling more panicky and overwhelmed. By now, the feelings had gripped her body: She could not sleep, eat, or sit still. When she was not shaking, she was vomiting—which made it harder to eat because she could not keep food down. She tried another therapist who said she was too anxious for treatment and another who complained that she was resisting treatment. Because she was so accomplished professionally, it did not occur to anyone that she might be suffering from trauma or from trauma-related dissociation.

UNDERSTANDING YOUR DIAGNOSIS

Because the theory of Structural Dissociation describes a way of understanding personality in chronically traumatized individuals, it is consistent with a number of diagnoses given by mental health professionals, including Complex PTSD (C-PTSD), Borderline Personality Disorder (BPD), Dissociative Identity Disorder (DID), and Dissociative Disorder Not Otherwise Specified (DDNOS). If you have ever been given any of these diagnoses, just remember that they are all diagnostic labels commonly given to trauma survivors who survived by fragmenting. They do not mean that you have a mental illness. Here is how to understand these diagnoses as manifestations of the parts.

If you have been given a diagnosis of BPD (the most common diagnosis for fragmented individuals), it simply means that you have a very strong cry for help part and a very strong fight part, making it difficult for you to tolerate separation, isolation, disappointment, and loneliness (the cry for help part)—and also making it difficult for you to tolerate anger and impulses to hurt yourself (the fight part) when someone has upset the cry for help part. You might function well at work or as a parent, or you might find these parts getting triggered even in those domains, making your job even harder.

If you have been given the diagnosis of a dissociative disorder, it means that you have more clearly observable compartmentalization and more experiences of being possessed by the emotions and impulses of the parts (e.g., the intense anger of the fight part or the hopelessness and shame of the submit part). But even if you do not understand why these strong feelings take hold so quickly and either blame yourself or the other person, you are conscious of what you have said or done.

If you have been given a diagnosis of DID, not only is the number of trauma-related parts likely to be greater, but you are more likely to have resource parts serving the Going On with Normal Life self or its priorities, for example, a professional part, a parenting part, or a part with special talents or social skills (see Figure 7.4).

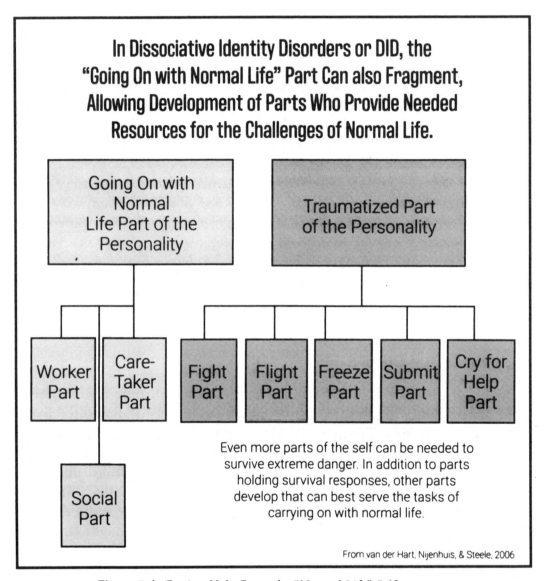

Figure 7.4: Getting Help From the "Normal Life" Self

Use **Worksheet 21: Signs of Structural Dissociation** to explore your own experience of fragmentation. Notice if it is helpful to think of the different reactions you commonly experience as reflective of different parts. Especially when you notice internal struggles or paradoxical reactions, be curious about a possible conflict between parts of you.

In addition, the parts of an individual with DID have a life of their own: They can take over the body and act outside of conscious awareness. The key indicator of DID is evidence that you have done or said things you do not recall. That is, you are not able to remember hours or days or particular activities in which you clearly have been engaged.

> *While updating her curriculum vitae, Celia, a successful organizational consultant, was surprised to discover that she had won an award in 1990 for which she had no memory. Not only could she not recall winning it, she could not recall what she had done to deserve it! She had long suspected she might have DID, but this discovery seemed to corroborate that idea. Annie also discovered disturbing evidence of her DID diagnosis when she received a letter from her oldest friend asking her never to contact him again under any circumstances. "I will never forgive you for what you said to me last week—it was cruel, and I don't want to be hurt anymore." Lacking a memory of having spoken to him recently, she could not imagine why she had been angry at him or what she could have said.*

RECOGNIZING SIGNS AND SYMPTOMS OF STRUCTURAL DISSOCIATION

The Structural Dissociation Model predicts that symptoms of fragmentation, depersonalization, out-of-body experiences, failures of integration, and internal conflict between parts of the personality are all to be expected as a legacy of traumatic experience, in addition to the more common symptoms of PTSD like flashbacks or numbing.

If you are not sure whether structural dissociation applies to you, start by seeing if the following more general points are issues or challenges in your life:

- **Limited benefit from therapy.** You have sought help from therapists, but therapy has not resulted in much progress or clarity. Or, worse yet, the therapies have been rocky, tumultuous, or overwhelming rather than supportive and helpful, or your symptoms have gotten more severe rather than lessening.
- **Somatic symptoms.** You have unusual pain tolerance or unusual sensitivity to pain, get migraine headaches, or have an unusual need for sleep but never feel rested. You have suffered at times from dizziness, nausea, and/or vomiting, and psychiatric medications have never worked well for you (either the side effects were too difficult or the drugs simply did not work).
- **Memory symptoms.** You have difficulty remembering how time was spent in a day or find that you have engaged in conversations or activities that other people recall but you do not. Perhaps you have suffered from blackouts, even when you were not drinking or taking drugs, or you often get lost even while driving somewhere familiar, such as going home from work. You might find yourself suddenly forgetting how to do something very simple and familiar.
- **Subtle manifestations of fragmentation.** You function well at work or as a parent while often or occasionally feeling overwhelmed, abandoned, depressed, ashamed, or suicidal and self-destructive.

If any of these points apply to you, it is quite possible that you may be dealing with structural dissociation. The core challenge for structurally dissociated individuals is the effect of trauma-related triggers on their fragmented parts. Triggers lead to trauma-related hijacking of the Going On with Normal Life part by other parts, resulting in internal struggles between the trauma-related parts and the Going On with Normal Life part. For example, accomplishing your "To-Do" list for the day is limited by a part's fear of leaving the house, or your wishes for more closeness and friendship are countered by the fight part's mistrust of anyone with whom you have a relationship. These inner struggles will be reflected in a series of difficulties thinking, making decisions, and managing your symptoms and impulses. The following is a more specific list detailing the different ways in which the presence of structurally dissociated parts can manifest in your life:

- **Evidence of child parts.** At times, you feel small and your body language young, whatever your chronological age. Sometimes you suddenly lose the ability to speak, worry a lot about being rejected and abandoned, have difficulty being alone, or need help in accomplishing basic activities (e.g., shopping, cooking, driving, turning on the computer).

- **Patterns of indecision.** You find it difficult to make even small, everyday decisions and to commit to activities, relationships, or jobs. You may have noticed a pattern of committing and then changing your mind or starting out a new job or relationship very easily, then having things fall apart. You are sometimes very responsible, especially to others, and at other times very irresponsible, usually to yourself.

- **Patterns of self-destructive and addictive behavior.** Despite your commitment to your family or job or to living, you find yourself engaging in behavior that you would never choose. For example, your Going On with Normal Life self might swear not to do any more binge-eating at night—and then, hours later, you might find yourself halfway through a pint of ice cream.

- **Difficulty "being here, now—in the present moment."** While your Going On with Normal Life self tries to avoid thinking about the past, the trauma-related parts are chronically preoccupied with danger, fearful, angry, sad, or lonely.

- **Difficulty soothing or even managing** the overwhelming emotions and impulses of the parts. Even when your normal life is a very safe and stable one, trauma-related parts may interpret traumatic triggers as signs that they are in the same danger of being annihilated, humiliated, or abandoned as they were in childhood.

Had Geraldine been given this information about structural dissociation, she would have resonated with the model. The fear and vulnerability she was experiencing did not feel like the person she knew herself to be. But no therapist seemed to be able to help her understand it or remedy what was happening. In the midst of what she termed her "nervous breakdown," Geraldine discovered something that helped: pain medication. After a tooth extraction, she was given an opioid pain medication that not only relieved her physical pain but also calmed her body and made the emotions bearable. Soon, she was using the pain medication daily and then multiple times a day. She was addicted but without knowing it because it was a behavior driven by her flight part and, although she was conscious of doing it, the thought that the pills would harm her never crossed the mind of her Going On with Normal Life self. Had her daughter been taking the same drugs, she would have known it was risky behavior, but because the drug-taking was the impulse of her flight part, she was not fully connected to it.

When trauma-related parts are triggered, each one responds with characteristic behaviors reflecting the different animal defenses, as you can see in Figure 7.5. The freeze part might become agoraphobic; the submit part may retreat to bed in shame, depression, and hopelessness; and the hypervigilant fight part might push people away with irritability, mistrust, or guardedness. Suicidal or self-harming parts that once increased the child's sense of having some control ("If it gets too bad, I can die. I can go to sleep and never wake up") may continue to have strong self-destructive impulses when triggered by threat, loss, or vulnerability—even tolerating the vulnerability of other parts may be difficult for fight parts. The flight response might drive addictive behavior, eating disorders, sexual addiction, and other sources of relief (or "flight") from the overwhelming trauma-related feelings and sensations. And then, in response to the acting out of fight-or-flight parts, submissive and needy parts might become ashamed, depressed, and filled with self-loathing, while the cry for help parts beg not to be abandoned. Often, survivors are left feeling confused, helpless, and even overwhelmed by all these different feelings and responses. Life feels more out of control, not less.

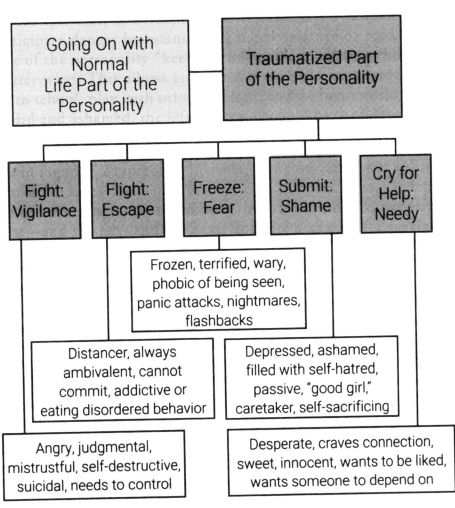

Figure 7.5: Figuring Out Who I Am

Use **Worksheet 22: Speaking the Language of Parts** to practice speaking the language of parts and unblending from the parts' feelings and impulses. Use the left-hand column to identify the feelings or reactions you notice in yourself and the right-hand column to translate those feelings into the language of parts.

PREPARING TO WORK WITH TRAUMA-RELATED DISSOCIATION AND FRAGMENTED PARTS

As we have learned in the previous chapters, scientific research on traumatic remembering tells us that both spontaneous triggering and deliberate recollecting result in activation of the autonomic nervous system and deactivation of the prefrontal cortex or thinking brain (van der Kolk, 2014). We *feel* endangered but have lost the ability to discriminate the actual degree of threat. Repeated reactivation of our survival responses (fear, shame, loss of breath, body tension, pulling back, collapsing, rage, the impulse to hide, even feelings of worthlessness and fault) increasingly sensitize the brain and body to respond to traumatic reminders even *more* automatically. It can become a vicious circle—one made worse when not only the body but also the trauma-related parts are triggered.

To address the challenges of fragmentation and break this vicious circle, we must first be able to "turn on" the prefrontal cortex. Without the noticing brain, it becomes impossible to do the work of trauma recovery. Use the diagrams and worksheets in this book to keep reminding yourself about triggers and triggering, the window of tolerance, and the Structural Dissociation Model. Keeping in mind and practicing the following suggestions can help you make use of your prefrontal cortex to observe trauma-related parts rather than getting swept away by their emotions or impulses:

1. **Assume that your intense and intrusive emotions, thoughts, and impulses are communications from parts**, as are numbing and loss of energy. That might be an oversimplification, but it is safer than assuming that all distress reflects your entire self feeling hurt, angry, ashamed, or afraid. Children and adults deal differently with distress. As adults, we have more ways to soothe or manage our emotions and more self-control over how we express ourselves. The traumatized child parts have no way to deal with distress other than to act or react, and they have no ability to reality test their actual level of safety.

   If the parts interpret traumatic activation as danger and so do you, it will keep reinforcing their sense of threat. However, when we identify distress as communication from a younger part of ourselves, we can change our relationship to the feelings or impulses or to the lack of feeling. We can be more curious and interested instead of overwhelmed and, as we know, curiosity helps to increase activity in the prefrontal cortex. Recognizing that your mind and body are being influenced moment by moment by emotional and physiological input from these trauma-related parts also stimulates the thinking brain. Once you can recognize the signs that parts are being triggered, your thinking brain begins to work better, your nervous system calms, and you can begin to soothe and bring hope to the parts.

2. **Practice differentiating your Going On with Normal Life self from your traumatized parts.** If we are now chronologically of adult age, every one of us has an adult self, no matter how depleted, demoralized, or unable to function we may feel. You might have little consciousness of your Going On with Normal Life self because your attention has been drawn to the overwhelming emotions or incomprehensible behavior of the parts, over which you feel no control. Or you may be aware of certain skills associated with being an adult, such as the ability to think, acquire knowledge and skills, or care for others or accomplish tasks, but experience these states as a false self rather than as a more stable, thoughtful, functioning self.

   Often it helps to simply identify what roles the Going On with Normal Life part plays in your life now—for example, going to work, taking care of a child, interfacing with the external world, doing things with friends, and participating in hobbies. Even if you feel incompetent and fraudulent, take it on faith that any of these activities are evidence that your Going On with Normal Life self is alive and well.

Then start to notice what is *not* that self—for example, when you feel small and overwhelmed at work or hopeless and depressed when out for a celebratory dinner with a friend or partner. Learn to assume that vulnerable feelings must logically belong to a part that feels much younger and more overwhelmed, such as a traumatized child part. When you feel angry and get sarcastic with your boss, is that your Going On with Normal Life self? What part would feel angry at an authority figure and not care about the consequences? At what age and stage of life would that be a characteristic behavior or way of thinking? At what age would we be worried about abandonment or not being loved? As you begin to differentiate what actions and reactions go with your Going On with Normal Life self and which go with different ages and stages of childhood, you will begin to better understand your traumatized selves. They have not been complicating your life intentionally. They get triggered, and their emotions, actions, and reactions are driven by fear, not maliciousness. Like any adult, the Going On with Normal Life part's job is to keep the younger generation feeling safe, stable, and protected—a job that always begins with understanding. When children or child parts feel heard and understood, they feel safer.

3. **Speak the language of parts.** Practicing the language of parts and interpreting symptoms, conflicts, intrusive emotions, impulsive behavior, or an inability to act as communications from parts simplifies the task of noticing the moment-to-moment responses of the parts and being curious. In addition, it aids in developing another important skill called "unblending" (Schwartz & Sweezy, 2020). As human beings get flooded by the emotional reactions of their parts, most of us "blend" with them. We tend to use "I" language, which strengthens the parts' reactions and our identification with them and increases the likelihood that we will act on their feelings and impulses. We feel the anxiety, anger, or shame and name it as *my* feeling—for example, "I feel very anxious today" or "I feel very depressed." Then we attempt to interpret the feeling based on the present context: "I think it's because I have this job interview coming up." Often, we base our actions on how we have interpreted the communications from the parts: "Maybe I should cancel the job interview—but I really need a job."

> *Guiliana repeatedly found herself attracted to unavailable men (her "attach for survival" part) and repulsed (the fight and flight parts) by men who were clearly attracted to her, especially those who were kind and wanted closeness. Although Guiliana was generally very tactful in her Going On with Normal Life self, she found herself pushing away the available men with an air of boredom or disgust (the fight part) while always finding reasons to excuse the unavailable men (the attach part). At other times, she felt alone and lonely. At age 45, she longed for a partner and home. However, because she automatically blended with whatever part was reacting in a given moment, she could not resolve the endless internal conflict about relationships until she began to name each different response as a part: "A part of me appreciates how patient and loving Dennis is with me, something I've always wanted. Another part of me finds him boring, and there's also a part who complains that she's not attracted to him at all. And how can I be with a man to whom I'm not attracted? I tend to believe that, so then I have to remember how attracted to him I was when we*

first met—and most of all to remember what I want in a relationship, which is love and respect."

If we use parts language, it will be easier to notice that it is the parts that are struggling. Saying, "I am depressed" seems to confirm that the whole body and mind are depressed, whereas saying, "A part of me is depressed" expresses empathy for the part while also conveying that there are other parts that are not depressed. Parts language also facilitates increased self-compassion: If an angry, lonely, or ashamed feeling is reframed as a communication from a young part, we can feel more empathy for those feelings.

In order to teach clients about blending and unblending, it is necessary to take on a very different role as a therapist. Instead of empathizing with trauma-related emotions and helping clients to sit with them, we need to help traumatized individuals first learn to mindfully *distance* from emotions; become curious about them as implicit, nonverbal memories held by a part; and then use parts language to be curious about distressing emotions: "She is anxious because it's getting dark so early in the day now." By learning to recognize that you are blended and then unblending, you can begin to make more sense of your internal struggles and avoid decisions or conclusions based on the input of a single part or group of parts.

Sometimes clients are told by professionals not to use the language of parts because it will make the dissociation or fragmentation worse. That concern would be understandable if it were true, but when we notice thoughts, feelings, and physical reactions, and name them as manifestations of parts, we are actually promoting what is called *integrative activity* in the brain. We cannot integrate aspects of ourselves if we have not observed and differentiated them as parts of our whole.

LEARNING TO HELP YOUR PARTS

The next step is to become more skilled at helping or soothing your parts. These are just a few of many ways of helping your nervous system and your parts to feel less overwhelmed, less reactive, or less numb. As traumatic reactions become less intense, your reactions to triggers (and theirs!) will slowly lessen:

- **Use your 10% solutions from Worksheet 15.** See which ones seem to be most helpful to the **parts**, not just to you.

- **Learn to use somatic resources** from Sensorimotor Psychotherapy (Ogden & Fisher, 2015) to regulate your nervous system and help all the parts. For example, feeling your feet on the floor can communicate to the parts that you are grounded even though they are freaking out. Placing a hand over your heart might signal to frightened or lonely parts that someone supportive is there. Lengthening your spine and slightly raising your chin might help to communicate hope to hopeless parts or decrease the shame of a part that feels worthless.

- **Practice the eight "C" qualities** from Internal Family Systems (Schwartz, 2001) illustrated in Figure 7.6. No matter how much trauma we have experienced, all human beings have the capacity to be curious, calm, clear, compassionate, creative, courageous, connected, and confident. The "C" qualities are never lost. Often, simply asking a part to step back or to sit back mobilizes the "C" qualities spontaneously, but it is also helpful to simply try to be more curious, more compassionate toward the parts, and more creative or calm in dealing with them.

- **Learn how to foster internal communication and cooperation.** Traumatized parts have no reason to trust any human being, and they will not trust your Going On with Normal Life self without some relationship building and a sense that you are there with them and for them. Practice talking to yourself (e.g., to them) by asking them simple questions, "What are you worried about if _____? How will it help to die? How will feeling hopeless help me?" Assume that the parts always have good intentions and that they are just trying to help you survive in a world they perceive as dangerous. Do not try to connect the parts to particular events. They developed to help you survive those events, but it is important to remember that *the parts are survival-related, not event-related.*

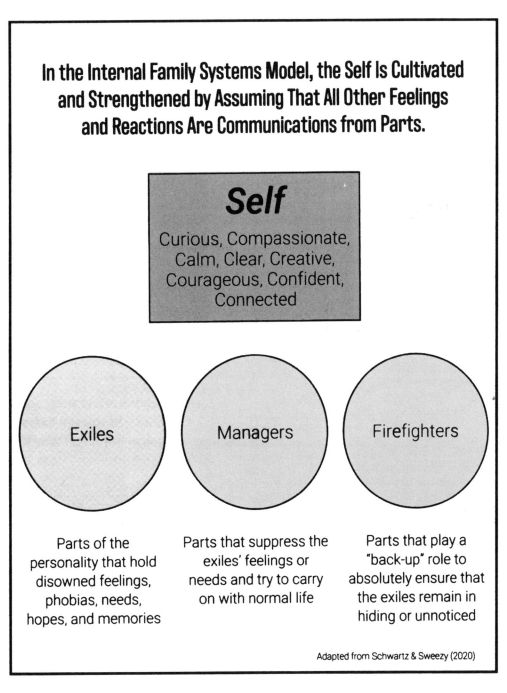

In the Internal Family Systems Model, the Self Is Cultivated and Strengthened by Assuming That All Other Feelings and Reactions Are Communications from Parts.

Self
Curious, Compassionate, Calm, Clear, Creative, Courageous, Confident, Connected

Exiles

Managers

Firefighters

Parts of the personality that hold disowned feelings, phobias, needs, hopes, and memories

Parts that suppress the exiles' feelings or needs and try to carry on with normal life

Parts that play a "back-up" role to absolutely ensure that the exiles remain in hiding or unnoticed

Adapted from Schwartz & Sweezy (2020)

Figure 7.6: The Eight "C" Qualities

Use **Worksheet 23: Strengthening Your "C" Qualities** to explore, recognize, and strengthen your "C" qualities. If you think you do not have a certain quality, ask yourself, "Have I ever been curious [or compassionate or courageous] for even one minute in my whole life?" We do not have to use these qualities to possess them, and the worksheet is meant to help grow your "C" qualities so they are resources for you.

For trauma to feel like a past experience, we need to have gained the ability to stay conscious and present even in the face of triggers, to tolerate the ups and downs of a normal life, and to help all parts feel safe in the body. This takes time and practice, but once you can be here now and help the parts join you, the trauma will feel over and you will be able to experience it as something that happened long ago.

Each time you notice how a feeling is linked to a particular part—each time you attach an age or state of mind to that part, feel curious about it, or connect it to current triggers—you are helping yourself to see all the aspects of your whole. You are not rejecting or ignoring some parts and feeling proud of other parts—you are welcoming every side and aspect of yourself. You are setting the stage for healing and resolution to take place, as we will see in the next chapter.

The Structural Dissociation Model

How old were you when the first traumas happened?
_____
_____
_____
_____

Pre-traumatic Personality

Going On with Normal Life Part of the Personality

Traumatized Part of the Personality

Describe some of the things you do that reflect this side of you, like taking care of your home, managing bills and chores, etc.

_____

_____

_____

_____

Describe how you can tell when you are in this side of yourself, like being afraid or angry or not wanting to see anyone.

_____

_____

_____

_____

Identifying the Traumatized Parts

When many traumatic events happen, more splitting is required to allow parts who can defend in different ways against the dangers the individual faces.

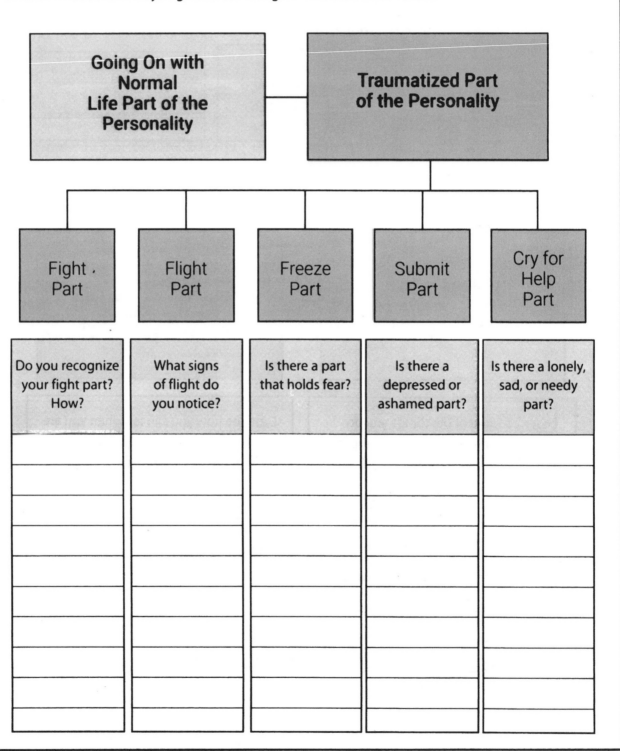

Going On with Normal Life Part of the Personality	Traumatized Part of the Personality			
Fight Part	**Flight Part**	**Freeze Part**	**Submit Part**	**Cry for Help Part**
Do you recognize your fight part? How?	What signs of flight do you notice?	Is there a part that holds fear?	Is there a depressed or ashamed part?	Is there a lonely, sad, or needy part?

Signs of Structural Dissociation

You might notice different sides of you in the descriptions below. Check any that apply and, in the column to the right, note to which part the feeling or behavior might belong.

- ☐ Able to function in some situations but not in others   _____
- ☐ Overwhelming emotions   _____
- ☐ Sudden intense physical or emotional reactions   _____
- ☐ Often feeling out of control of what I do and say   _____
- ☐ Anxiety rules my life   _____
- ☐ Feeling "possessed"   _____
- ☐ Can't stop hurting myself   _____
- ☐ Can't stop drinking or using drugs   _____
- ☐ Having plans for the future but not wanting to live   _____
- ☐ Feeling out of control of my body   _____
- ☐ Can never make a decision   _____
- ☐ Insecure about acceptance by others   _____
- ☐ Can't trust anyone or trust too easily   _____
- ☐ Fears of abandonment   _____
- ☐ "All over the place"   _____
- ☐ Depression rules my life   _____
- ☐ Hating myself   _____
- ☐ Anger rules my life   _____
- ☐ Shame rules my life   _____
- ☐ Pushing other people away   _____
- ☐ Too dependent, too needy   _____
- ☐ Not knowing who I am anymore   _____
- ☐ Having trouble with my memory   _____

What is it like when you think of these different reactions as communications from different parts of you?

_____

_____

Speaking the Language of Parts

Use the left-hand column to identify feelings or reactions you might be having and the right-hand column to translate the feelings into parts language.

Feeling or Reaction   **Translation**

☐ "I'm depressed."   ☐ _____

☐ "I am a failure."   ☐ _____

☐ "I want to die."   ☐ _____

☐ "It's hopeless."   ☐ _____

☐ "I'm worthless."   ☐ _____

☐ "No one loves me."   ☐ _____

☐ "I want to hurt myself."   ☐ _____

☐ "I'm fine."   ☐ _____

☐ "I just need a stiff drink."   ☐ _____

☐ "I just want all this to be over."   ☐ _____

☐ "I don't trust anyone."   ☐ _____

☐ "I am so angry I feel like
    could explode."   ☐ _____

Notice if it feels different when you express the feeling or thought in parts language:

_____

_____

Strengthening Your "C" Qualities

Use this worksheet to write down the "C" qualities you have and where you have them in your life. Think of some ways you can strengthen these qualities.

Self

Curious, Compassionate, Calm, Clear, Creative,
Courageous, Confident, Connected

Curiosity: _____

Compassion: _____

Calm: _____

Clarity/Perspective: _____

Creativity: _____

Courage: _____

Confidence: _____

Connection: _____

Remember: Any thought, feeling, impulse, or physical reaction that does not possess any of the "C" qualities is always a communication from a part!

8

Healing and Resolution

Post-traumatic stress represents our biological inheritance as human mammals. After trauma, our survival instincts keep the mind and body riveted on the past. The visual images play and replay. Our senses become heightened to detect potential danger, and we react to sounds, sights, and other human beings in anticipation that they will be threatening. All our emotional and physical reactions become heightened as well; we might find ourselves reacting more intensely or, conversely, not reacting at all. Suddenly, we feel excruciating shame, lose the capacity for speech, or comply when every fiber of our being wants to say, "No!" Often, we either become overwhelmed by what we sense or feel, or we are inexplicably numb and everything is an effort. Sometimes, there is no predicting how we will react to anything.

Trauma leaves behind little to no sense that an event occurred and that it had a beginning, a middle, and then an end. There is no visceral feeling of relief at having survived. The past has not been resolved or integrated with a clear felt sense that "the traumatic event is over—it is behind me—and I survived it." Even decades afterward, traumatized individuals can still be frozen in time midway through the traumatic experience—afraid, overwhelmed, numb, ashamed, or helplessly furious—without any awareness that they have long ago made it safely to the other side. You might know intellectually that it is over but still not feel safe or feel normal because the trauma is still alive in your body and nervous system. Given that the story has had no ending, how do survivors achieve a sense of completion or resolution?

ACKNOWLEDGING THE PAST WHILE STAYING CONNECTED TO THE PRESENT

For decades, experts believed that the experience of resolution could only be gained by remembering the traumatic events and reexperiencing the unresolved emotions until they felt over. A logical belief to be sure, but it was a treatment approach that often produced the opposite effect on trauma survivors: shame instead of relief, an increase in overwhelming feelings and self-hatred, and impulses to attack their bodies or end their lives. In the 40 years since the inception of the trauma field, experts in the field and survivors have learned the hard way that reexperiencing the past is equally or more likely to contribute to a *failure* of resolution.

Now we know that, for trauma treatment to be effective, no matter what methods we employ, survivors *do not* have to reexperience or even remember the past. However, they *do* have to be able to experience some kind of clear physical and emotional sense that "it" is over and that they are still here. We must be able to acknowledge the past and reflect on its legacy without reexperiencing it. Even when trauma responses keep demanding our attention, we have to learn how to access other places in our minds and to use the resources of our bodies and minds to change the physical responses that keep us traumatized.

If the goal of trauma treatment is "to be here instead of there," as Bessel van der Kolk tells us, any therapeutic approach must directly or indirectly keep the emphasis on the present. Although this book is not a substitute for trauma-informed treatment, it is intended to provide the building blocks to help you connect to a felt sense of safety in the present moment. This may seem like a simple task, but it is not. The difficulty is that, as you now know, the implicit or nonverbal aspects of memory keep reactivating the sense of immediate danger. When we remember a traumatic event, or when we are triggered by some small cue in the here and now, our bodies automatically begin to mobilize for danger, not knowing that we are remembering threat rather than being threatened now. And when the prefrontal cortex shuts down and our bodies go into survival mode, we cannot rationally analyze what we are feeling.

> *Week after week, Annie reported, "It's bad—everything is falling apart. There is too much stress in my life. Nothing has changed." But when I inquired about what was happening, she reported, "I thought I was going to have a quiet afternoon, but my goddaughter called and wanted a ride to her job ... It's almost autumn—and I'm not ready for winter ... We haven't had a single party or cookout all summer—no one comes to our house anymore." With further discussion, it emerged that her goddaughter's need for rides triggered an anticipatory wariness that she was being used; the tasks of putting away garden hoses, getting ready to rake leaves, and cleaning out gutters on her house felt like emergencies that had to be addressed immediately; and the slowing of family social occasions as her children moved into their 30s triggered feelings of being unwanted and unimportant. These normal life stresses had triggered disconnected feeling memories of being used, on the brink of disaster, and painfully alone.*

Resolution of the past requires transforming our relationship to what happened, and this is achieved through the development of the following skills, all of which have been covered throughout the previous chapters:

- Expanding the window of tolerance until both the implicit memories and the day-to-day stresses of a life after trauma can be experienced as within our capacity. We do not have to *like* trauma-related feelings, past or present, but we do need to feel a sense of being able to *tolerate* them. If we have the bandwidth to stay present, manage our impulses and emotions, and keep our thinking brains online, we do not have to reexperience overwhelming feelings or go numb.

- Recognizing as implicit memory the feeling and bodily states that can still be triggered even after successful treatment, whether or not we have the images or the narrative of an event.

- Learning to recognize triggering stimuli and to accurately label triggered states as responses to the past ("This is a feeling memory or a body memory," "This is triggering"), refraining from searching for proof beyond a reasonable doubt about what happened, and not trying to remember every detail of what you know at your core has happened.

- Identifying distressing feelings or symptoms as survival strategies rather than as problems or defects to be eliminated.

For all of these reasons, I have focused attention in this book on helping you notice when your body and brain are remembering dangers from the past. And when we can finally appreciate what it took to adapt to that dangerous environment and to parents who were incapable of safe attachment, then it becomes possible to live fully in the present despite traumatic triggering and trauma-related conditioning. It becomes possible to have a healing story, a story that makes meaning of what happened and that attests to how we have survived it.

> *Annie's sense of emergency about household and yard tasks was a body memory of the danger she and her siblings faced if they did not complete their chores on time. The anticipatory prediction that she was being used was the feeling memory of a child who, over and over again, was used sexually, physically, and emotionally by the adults in her life. And her inability to say "no" reflected the conditioned learning that it was safer to help her alcoholic mother manage her life than to wait until her mother felt stressed. The traumatic past had been over for over 40 years, but it did not feel over.*

OVERCOMING THE CHALLENGES TO RESOLUTION

Bessel van der Kolk (2014) gives us a simple prescription for trauma treatment: Recovery is a process of "re-establishing ownership of one's mind and body" (p. 203). And he lists four steps to that goal:

1. "Finding a way to become calm and focused;
2. Learning to maintain that calm [despite triggers] that remind you of the past;
3. Finding a way to be fully alive in the present and engaged with the people around you;
4. Not having to keep secrets from yourself, including secrets about the ways that you have managed to survive." (pp. 203-204)

"Finding a way to become calm and focused" is another way of saying that resolving trauma requires expanding the window of tolerance, just as we discussed in Chapter Three. Increasing the number of 10% solutions in your repertoire and learning to use them when triggers activate the nervous system, emotions, and body gradually increases the sense of being okay in the present. When you are in the present, even just noticing "I'm triggered" over and over again, you are more available to focus on work, play, rest, relationships, and enjoyment. And as the window of tolerance expands, most individuals gradually feel less triggered in their daily lives and relationships, or they are more easily able to recover from having been triggered.

A life after trauma is not a life in which we will never ever be triggered again. It is a life in which being triggered is a nuisance, not a catastrophe or an experience of shame. A nuisance just requires patience and perspective, the ability to "maintain that calm [despite triggers] that remind you of the past," which becomes a less effortful step as we have more capacity or bandwidth.

> *Annie was reflecting on how far she had come in her recovery but often still experienced her life as unsatisfying, grim, lonely, and meaningless. I asked her to be curious for a moment about this pattern. "How might this have helped*

you survive? What if your body learned to block any good feelings or sense of pride to protect you?"

She pondered this question, "Well, I do remember my mother seemed to be triggered when we were happy and definitely when we accomplished anything—it's like she was jealous of her children's successes—and she would become more abusive." Then she recalled, "And we couldn't let down our guards—we couldn't afford to relax. There were so many people in our lives who might do something to us at any moment. We couldn't afford to feel safe, calm, or loved." It felt right, and it felt true. "So, even though there are people in my life who love me," she reflected, "I can't enjoy it... And even when I have a good day or I do something good, I can't feel good about it. That's amazing! So, it's not my life that's the problem; it's how my body helped me to survive!"

If we can identify when we are triggered, it becomes possible to "be fully alive in the present and engaged with the people around [us]" (van der Kolk, 2014, p. 204). If we can keep noticing the signs of triggering—the triggers, the body sensations, and the emotions—as just memory or just sensations, their effects do not linger. Most of all, the ability to just notice the experience of being triggered, rather than react to it, is an act of self-acceptance. "I'm triggered because I experienced trauma, not because I am a bad or flawed human being." By accepting the experiences of being triggered as normal, we accept ourselves as normal, recognize that we are doing the best we can, and increase our awareness that being triggered is a badge of courage—a testament to being survivors of trauma.

However, self-acceptance is not easy. Perhaps the most difficult hurdle for many trauma survivors is overcoming the self-hatred and self-alienation often necessitated by abuse and neglect. Small children with no way to explain what is happening to them blame, shame, silence, and reject themselves—all of which help to lessen the danger. A child (or adult) who blames herself and then feels shame has no trouble being seen and not heard, finds it easier to comply and collapse, and less difficult to have no needs or opinions. But that ingenious adaptation when we are young becomes a hurdle in recovery. Once the danger is over, self-acceptance and self-compassion are necessary to help us do the work of recovery and allow the wounds to heal. That may be the inspiration for Bessel van der Kolk's final ingredient in the recipe for recovery: "Not having to keep secrets from yourself, including secrets about the ways that you have managed to survive" (van der Kolk, 2014, p. 204). By accepting that all living creatures are instinctively driven to survive by any means necessary, we can forgive ourselves for whatever we did to stay alive or to maintain some semblance of control. Acknowledging that it can require extreme measures to cope, adapt, and survive threatening conditions when we are young and without financial or emotional support is a way of saying, "That's how I survived; that is why I'm here now."

Justin endured years of abuse and abandonment by his mentally ill, substance-abusing parents until he was kicked out for "disobedience" and became a homeless adolescent. Out on the streets, he soon found that the only way to survive was by prostituting himself, but tolerating prostitution required being high. He quickly became addicted to heroin, thanks to a drug-dealing boyfriend, and even sold it at times of desperation. Deeply ashamed of this period in his life, he hid the secret from his friends and family even after he had fought his way back to sobriety and eventually to college. Thanks to his choice of psychology as a major, it slowly became easier to view this period in his life as just a way of surviving and to begin to feel some pride in himself for fighting his way back from the brink to a healthy, normal life. He now had a healing story: "How I survived wasn't pretty, but I did survive, and now I'm going to pay it forward."

LEARNING TO ORIENT TO THE PRESENT MOMENT

It is tragic that the very defensive responses that once helped to save our lives later prevent us from appreciating that we did survive. Many survivors of trauma long for relief, long for a sense of pride and confidence, long to feel unafraid and unashamed. But because the brain and body seem designed to prioritize anticipation of danger over the enjoyment that it is over, relief is often absent or short-lived. Our senses still orient to potential threat. Our bodies still mobilize defensive responses even with the subtlest of triggers. Resolution of trauma depends on the individual's ability to change those patterns. In Chapters Two through Five, we discussed and practiced many different ways of changing trauma-related responses. Go back to those chapters if you are feeling at a loss as to how to manage the incessant triggering and its disruptive effect.

One of the most important skills that will help at this stage of your recovery is what is known as *orienting* (Ogden & Fisher, 2015). The orienting reflex is familiar to all of us, so familiar that we rarely notice ourselves orienting even though we all do it constantly. We turn at the sound of our name or if we hear an unfamiliar or alarming sound. We pause when we go into a store, airport, or new building, and look around to see where to go. As parents, we are always orienting toward our children to make sure they are safe. "Where is he [or she]?" is a familiar parental question. We do the same with our pets. We instinctively orient toward potential danger first but also toward sources of nourishment, such as the produce section of the grocery store, or a friendly-looking stranger at a social gathering.

The instinctive trauma response of hypervigilance is a form of orienting: Our brains and bodies are constantly scanning for threat or danger. The feeling of mistrust is similar, as it mobilizes us to be attentive to any sign that a situation or individual cannot be trusted. Trust, on the other hand, requires us to focus our attention toward information that confirms the belief that we can trust. To resolve trauma requires that we learn to orient differently and more realistically. As long as hypervigilant orienting keeps us focused on threat, it is physically impossible to feel a sense that the past is over and things are safe now.

Annie hated her home, felt ashamed of it, and often expressed dread about returning home after therapy. She described it as a hovel, but I knew that description could not possibly be accurate given how many hours each week she and her husband spent maintaining their house and property. I asked her to imagine driving home after the therapy session and to pause as she visualized parking in the driveway and to then look around. "What do you see as you get out if the car?" I asked.

"I see a white farmhouse with a fence around it. And I can feel my body relaxing when I see the fence. It looks safe."

"Notice that fence and then notice what else your eyes are drawn to."

"I can see that everything is newly painted, and the back door is bright red. I painted it red to make it more inviting."

"How do you feel when you see the red door?"

"I feel warm, and it makes me want to go inside."

Room by room, I asked Annie to imagine walking through her home and to just notice whatever she saw. Finally, we came to her study. The study held deep meaning for her: Two years ago, she and her husband had decided that she needed a sanctuary in the home, a place where she could read, sew, or rest and where she would not be disturbed. But it had been triggering to actually convert the guest room into her study because it triggered beliefs that she was undeserving, that it would be taken away, and that she should not inconvenience others by allocating a whole room to herself. Nonetheless, she had done it.

As she imagined looking around her study and fully orienting to it, she could feel a strong somatic sense of being in the here and now. "This is my room—with the colors I like, with the quilt I made up on the wall, and with my desk by the window." She had a sense of awe and pleasure, along with an awareness of how different this room was than the rooms of her childhood home; it was orderly, colorful, and homey. In the weeks that followed, she practiced orienting to her study each time she was triggered. She might feel anxious, ashamed, or overwhelmed, but when she looked around the study (or even visualized looking around), she felt her body calming and an awareness that here, in her new home, she was safe—so safe she even had a room of her very own.

It can be very challenging to learn to orient to what is positive when your body instinctively responds to the environment as a threat. It does not happen all by itself unfortunately. It takes repeated practice: orienting to non-threatening or positive stimuli, expanding the window of tolerance, deliberately choosing to focus on what feels good, and working with the fear and shame connected to the experience of positive feelings.

APPRECIATING SURVIVAL: THE FOUR STEPS TO FREEDOM

Annie once said, *"I'm glad I became who I am… I'm not glad about all that trauma, and I wish it had never happened, but I would not be the person I am without it."*

A life after trauma has to include some sense of pride, respect, or just awe that we have survived. We might have to thank those parts of us that contributed to our survival, even if how they (or we) survived is not pretty. The sense that we have been through a dark time but now have made it out of the darkness is important for recovery. There is no conclusion to the story of trauma without knowing that we survived. But because post-traumatic responses seem to have developed to increase the odds of survival for early mankind, knowing that we have survived takes work!

Claudia Black's "Four Steps to Freedom" (1999, p. 47) provides simple steps for helping survivors work their way to freedom from the past. I have adapted these steps slightly for trauma survivors who might be triggered by remembrance of the past:

- **Step One.** Assume that whatever distress you might be experiencing has been triggered and is related to the childhood past. [*This is a leap of faith that is crucial to trauma recovery.*]

- **Step Two.** Connect that distress to its roots in the traumatic past by fast-forwarding through your childhood history and noticing where the feelings and body sensations you notice right now best fit. [*"Fast-forward" means no more than 20–30 seconds! Focusing on or thinking about the past for more than that short time risks activating the trauma responses.*]

- **Step Three.** Identify the internalized old belief that developed as a result of that experience. [*Ask yourself: "What would any human being come to believe about themselves in that situation?" Or think about the negative beliefs that most trouble you day to day and identify them as related to the past, not to you personally.*]

- **Step Four.** Find a way to challenge that old belief so that you can begin to develop new beliefs that better fit your life today. [*You are already challenging those beliefs the moment you label them as "old." That is the first sub-step. The next sub-step is to create a new possible belief, such as "I had to believe this in order to survive" or "This belief helped me to survive because it made me more_____."*] It is not necessary to come up with a new positive belief or to expect yourself to believe it. It is only necessary to challenge the old beliefs.

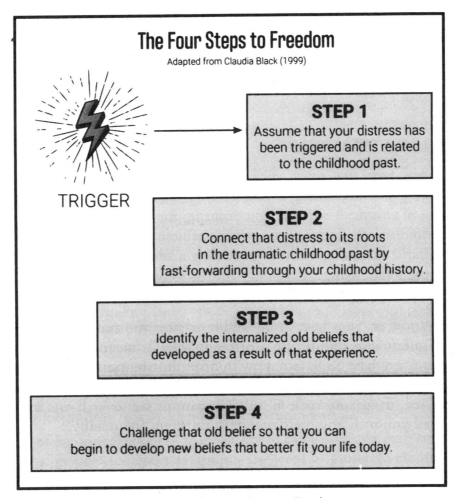

Figure 8.1: The Four Steps to Freedom

Without repeated practice of new reactions and new beliefs, the same responses that helped you survive will continue to be triggered over and over again. It appears that the brain and body are slower to let go of responses associated with survival under threat, and the only way to combat that phenomenon is to keep practicing the new responses until they become increasingly automatic. No wonder survivors and therapists alike held on so long to the belief that all it took to resolve trauma was to tell the story! It would have been far easier if the burden of traumatic experience were lifted just by sharing the secrets of the past.

> Use **Worksheet 24: The Four Steps to Freedom** whenever you find yourself being triggered.

However, practicing the Four Steps to Freedom is empowering. I recommend making several copies of the worksheets in this book so you can repeat them again and again—and that includes repeating the Four Steps whenever you are triggered. After practicing with the worksheets, you will find yourself increasingly able to recognize that you have been triggered, to trust that there is a connection to the past, and to assume that you are still carrying some conscious or unconscious belief as a result of that experience. Once we become aware of how these old beliefs are constricting our lives, it becomes easier and easier to challenge them.

But any time you find it difficult to challenge an old belief, be especially curious. If you find yourself saying, "But it's true!," assume that this automatic "no" reaction means that the belief once played an important role in your survival and, for that reason, your mind is not giving it up without a fight.

PHASES OF TRAUMA TREATMENT

Judith Herman has been the most vocal advocate of what is called *phase-oriented* trauma treatment—meaning that addressing overwhelming, terrifying, and sickening memories cannot safely be the focus of treatment without first ensuring the individual's safety and stability. Because post-traumatic responses challenge even a wide, resilient window of tolerance, it is often unsafe to dive into traumatic memories without providing a solid foundation. In fact, it can become a repetition of having to face danger as a small child without the emotional and physical resources to manage an overwhelming experience.

Once understood as "you have to be stable to face the trauma," we now understand the prioritization of safety and stability in a different way. It means the discovery that "you have to be here now and you have to be safe now in order for the trauma to feel *over*." It cannot feel over and done if you are in an abusive relationship, are harming yourself, are trying to die, or are addicted to "sex, drugs and rock 'n' roll." It cannot feel over if you are still taking care of those who harmed you or if you are dependent on them financially.

The following are the stages of trauma treatment, adapted from Judy Herman (1992), that you can see summarized in Figure 8.2.

STAGES OF TRAUMA TREATMENT
Adapted from Judith Herman (1992)

STAGE 1: Safety and Stabilization: Overcoming Dysregulation
Tasks:
- Establishment of bodily safety
- Establishment of a safe environment
- Establishment of emotional stability

Goal: To create a safe and stable life in the here and now

STAGE 2: Coming to Terms with Traumatic Memories
Tasks:
- Overcoming the fear of the traumatic events and body/emotional memories so they can be integrated
- In order to metabolize the nonverbal memories, making use of EMDR, hypnotherapy, or body-oriented therapies

Goal: To come to terms with the traumatic past

STAGE 3: Integration and Moving On
Tasks:
- Decreasing shame and self-alienation
- Developing a greater capacity for healthy attachment
- Taking up personal and professional goals reflecting posttraumatic meaning-making

Goal: To overcome fears of a normal life, healthy challenge and change, and intimacy

Figure 8.2: Phase-Oriented Trauma Treatment

STAGE 1: SAFETY AND STABILIZATION: OVERCOMING DYSREGULATION

As a first step, survivors must be taught to understand the effects of trauma, to recognize common symptoms, and to interpret the meaning of overwhelming body sensations, intrusive emotions, and distorted cognitive schemas. The achievement of safety and stability rests on the following tasks:

- Establishment of bodily safety (e.g., abstinence from self-injury, sobriety)
- Establishment of a safe environment (e.g., a secure living situation, non-abusive relationships, a job and/or regular income, adequate supports)
- Establishment of emotional stability (e.g., ability to calm the body, regulate impulses, self-soothe, and manage post-traumatic symptoms triggered by mundane events)

The goal of this stage is to create a safe and stable life in the here and now, allowing individuals to safely address the traumatic past, not relive it.

STAGE 2: COMING TO TERMS WITH TRAUMATIC MEMORIES

At this stage, the survivor works to overcome the fear of the traumatic events and body/emotional memories so they can be integrated, allowing appreciation for the person he or she has become as a result of the trauma. In order to metabolize the nonverbal memories, make use of EMDR (Shapiro, 2001); body-oriented therapies, like Sensorimotor Psychotherapy (Ogden & Fisher, 2015) and Somatic Experiencing (Levine, 2015); or Internal Family Systems therapy (Schwartz, 2001). Pacing ensures that individuals do not become stuck in avoidance or overwhelmed by memories and flashbacks. Since "remembering is not recovering," the goal is only to come to terms with the traumatic past, not to remember its details.

STAGE 3: INTEGRATION AND MOVING ON

The survivor can now begin to work on decreasing shame and self-alienation, developing a greater capacity for healthy attachment, and taking up personal and professional goals that reflect post-traumatic meaning-making. Overcoming fears of a normal life, healthy challenge and change, and intimacy become the focus of the work. As the survivor's life becomes reconsolidated around a healthy present and healed self, the trauma feels further away, part of an integrated understanding of the self, but no longer a daily focus.

> Use **Worksheet 25: In Which Phase of Recovery Are You?** to look at where you are in the phases of recovery.

Very important warning: Wherever you are in the stages of recovery, *do not* judge yourself! There are many reasons the process of recovery is slow, and none of them is about you. There is a huge international shortage of trauma specialists in the mental health and medical worlds. Perhaps you have not had specialized treatment or a trauma-trained therapist. Perhaps the therapist has been using the old "tell your story and it will be over" model. Perhaps you needed to fragment or dissociate to survive—an ingenious way of surviving that requires more time to resolve. Perhaps you have been afraid of treatment because you thought it meant having to remember and having to feel the emotions all over again. Maybe you wanted to believe it had never happened.

All these are normal problems that slow the process of recovery, but they do not prevent it. Even if you are afraid that you are not ready to even acknowledge what happened to you, do not give up! Look for a specialized trauma therapist and tell them in advance that you are looking for a therapist familiar with the work of Bessel van der Kolk, Pat Ogden, or myself. Make sure to be honest about how hard it is to even imagine addressing what happened.

Recovering from trauma is a complex and very slow process. Keep reminding yourself that the symptoms represent survival responses! Even trying to kill yourself is an attempt to take back control of your feelings and your future. Most likely, it is a memory of wanting to stop the violence and to end your suffering. Self-harm or drug use are not evidence of your defectiveness. Both bring immediate relief and, despite their harmful long-term effects, these may have been the only ways you knew to manage the overwhelming feelings. Try to admire your ingenuity, even if these ways of surviving have also led to shame and hopelessness.

Try not to judge yourself or worry about where you are in the process. Just focus on the next step, whether it be the establishment of a safe environment or the ability to acknowledge the past and experience triggering as remembering. We all find our way to healing step by step, and most of us will not recognize that we are there until well after our own personal legacy of trauma has been resolved and we have forgiven ourselves.

HEALING AND FORGIVENESS

Healing or feeling healed begins to happen the moment when we accept and forgive ourselves—the moment when we see that small child who we once were through the eyes of the compassionate adult we have become. That little boy or girl believed the feeling of shame was evidence that he or she was at fault, defective, or unworthy. Children are too young to know that shame is simply a survival response that helps us submit when we are trapped. Children do not know that it is safer to blame themselves than to blame the adults on whom they depend for a roof over their heads and something to eat. They do not know that, had they fought back, the violence would only have been worse. Be curious when hopelessness, shame, or anger continue to dominate your mind and body despite your hard work to transform the effects of the trauma. Ask yourself, "Why might my young self be afraid to believe that it's not his or her fault?" and "Why would a little boy or girl be afraid to hope?"

> Use **Worksheet 26: Welcoming Your Younger Selves** to begin the process of getting to know your child selves, which is the first step in making them welcome rather than trying to ignore, control, or reject their vulnerability.

When we can finally see how young we were, how magical our thinking was, and how ingeniously we survived, it is easier to open our hearts to that child we used to be.

And when we feel warmth, pride, or compassion for that little one inside, something important changes. We experience our grown-up selves in present time while simultaneously connecting to that wounded child who carries the emotional and somatic legacy of the past. In those moments, past and present come together, and the warmth of our compassion heals a little more of that child's fear, hurt, and loneliness—until the day we wake up and feel healed or normal at last. Be patient with the child parts who are afraid to believe they are not to blame, afraid to believe that they were ingenious and creative, afraid to believe that it will be safe now. Keep extending the same compassion you would offer to any vulnerable being until you feel that child inside relaxing, softening, or sitting up a little straighter. Know that when the young child inside you begins to feel the warmth and kindness of your acceptance and welcome, you are finally healing the legacy of the traumatic past.

The Four Steps to Freedom

✓ **Assume that the distress you are experiencing has been triggered and is related to the childhood past.**

Describe that distress (tears, hurt, anger, shame, hopelessness), and see what happens when you assume it is triggered and related to the past:

_____

_____

_____

✓ **Connect that distress to its roots in the traumatic past by fast-forwarding through your childhood history for 20–30 seconds and noticing where the feelings and body sensations best fit.**

Describe in just 1–2 sentences where the distress fits. Try to acknowledge where it might fit rather than trying to be sure:

_____

_____

_____

✓ **Identify the internalized old beliefs that developed as a result of that experience.**

Describe a belief or beliefs about yourself that resulted from how you were treated:

_____

_____

_____

✓ **Find a way to challenge that old belief so that you can begin to develop new beliefs that better fit your life today.**

Describe what happens when you label the belief as old. What would you like to believe now? What would you want a child in that situation to believe?

_____

_____

_____

In Which Phase of Recovery Are You?

STAGE 1: Safety and Stabilization

Ask yourself: Have I established **bodily safety?** (e.g., "I am sober, no longer hurt my body, I go to the doctor" vs. "I still self-injure, do drugs, and let my body be abused")

_____

_____

Have I established a **safe environment?** (e.g., a secure living situation, nonabusive relationships, I can earn enough to take care of myself)

_____

_____

Have I established **emotional stability?** (e.g., ability to calm the body, regulate impulses, self-soothe, manage triggering)

_____

_____

Do I have **a safe and stable life in the here and now?**

_____

_____

STAGE 2: Coming to Terms with Traumatic Memories

Ask yourself: Do I try to avoid the word _trauma_? Can I acknowledge the past? Or am I always focused on the past? Can I recognize when I am triggered? Or do I just go into the past without knowing I'm triggered? What triggers me most often? Do I know and appreciate how I survived?

_____

_____

STAGE 3: Integration and Moving On

Ask yourself: Does the trauma feel more finished? Am I less often triggered or quicker to recognize triggering? How has my relationship to other people changed? Has my relationship to myself changed? Do I still believe it was my fault? Or do I have more perspective? What good qualities or skills do I have as a result of what I went through? Has the trauma changed my goals in life?

_____

_____

Welcoming Your Younger Selves

Use this worksheet to develop a clearer picture of the child you were at **different ages and stages.** He or she does not have to be connected to any specific event—just to the environment as a whole at that age.

Younger Self

How old is this child?

What is his or her face and body language telling you?

What is this child thinking and feeling still?

When you see your younger self, notice how you feel toward him or her.

_____
_____
_____

If you notice a judgment or negative reaction, assume that the hostility comes from a different part. What do you notice about this part?

_____
_____
_____

What happens if you welcome this younger self as you would any child?

_____
_____
_____

Youngest Self

How old is this child?

What is his or her face and body language telling you?

What is this child thinking and feeling still?

What happens when you imagine and welcome your very youngest self?

_____
_____
_____

What happens if you welcome that part too?

_____
_____
_____

REFERENCES

For your convenience, you may download a pdf version of the worksheets in this book from our dedicated website: pesi.com/legacyoftrauma

Black, C. (1999). *Changing course: Healing from loss, abandonment, and fear.* Bainbridge Island, WA: MAC Publishing.

Fisher, J. (2017). *Healing the fragmented selves of trauma survivors: Overcoming internal self-alienation.* New York: Routledge.

Hanson, R. (2013). *Hardwiring happiness: The new brain science of contentment, calm, and confidence.* New York: Harmony Books.

Herman, J. (1992). *Trauma and recovery.* New York: W.W. Norton.

LeDoux, J. E. (2002). *The synaptic self: How our brains become who we are.* New York: Viking Press.

Levine, P. (2015). *Trauma and memory: Brain and body in search of the living past.* Berkeley, CA: North Atlantic Books.

Ogden, P., & Fisher, J. (2015). *Sensorimotor psychotherapy: Interventions for trauma and attachment.* New York: W. W. Norton.

Ogden, P., Minton, K., & Pain, C. (2006). *Trauma and the body: A sensorimotor approach to psychotherapy.* New York: W.W. Norton.

Perry, B. D., Pollard, R. A., Blakely, T. L., Baker, W. L., & Vigilante, D. (1995). Childhood trauma, the neurobiology of adaptation, and "use-dependent" development of the brain: How "states" become "traits." *Infant Mental Health Journal, 16*(4), 271–291.

Schwartz, R., & Sweezy, M. (2020). *Internal family systems therapy* (2nd ed.). New York: Guilford Press.

Schwartz, R. (2001). *Introduction to the internal family systems model.* Oak Park, IL: Trailhead Publications.

Shapiro, F. (2001). *Eye movement desensitization and reprocessing: Basic principles, protocols, and procedures* (2nd ed.). New York: Guilford Press.

Siegel, D. J. (1999). *The developing mind: Toward a neurobiology of interpersonal experience.* New York: Guilford Press.

van der Hart, O., Nijenhuis, E. R. S., & Steele, K. (2006). *The haunted self: Structural dissociation and the treatment of chronic traumatization.* New York: W.W. Norton.

van der Kolk, B. A., & Fisler, R. (1995). Dissociation and the fragmentary nature of traumatic memories: Overview and exploratory study. *Journal of Traumatic Stress, 8*(4), 505–525.

van der Kolk, B. A. (2014). *The body keeps the score: Brain, mind, and body in the treatment of trauma.* New York: Viking Press.